KANUGA

Story of a Gathering Place

Jack Reak

Jack Reak

Foreword by Joe Cumming

Published by Kanuga Conferences, Inc.
Postal Drawer 250
Hendersonville, North Carolina 28793

Printed in the United States of America

First Edition, 1993
First Printing, 1993

Library of Congress Catalogue Card Number: 93-80360
Reak, Jack
Kanuga—Story of a Gathering Place
Editors: Albert S. Gooch, Jr.
Sara T. Dudney
Emily H. Freeman

ISBN 0-9639021-0-5

This book was printed by CBS Printers, Charlotte,
North Carolina.
Cover and jacket design by Emily H. Freeman

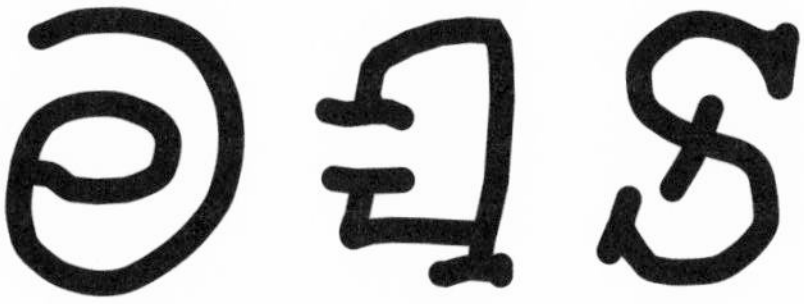

Foreword

It was the third week of Guest Period, 1993. The announcement at lunch told us that a Jack Reak would be in the chapel at 4 p.m. to talk about—and show slides from—his soon-to-be-published history of Kanuga.

History of Kanuga?!

My sister Nancy Connolly and I had the same reaction from different tables in the dining room. We bristled. Who was this Jack Reak and how dare he write a history of Kanuga without consulting us.

We have been coming here since 1932. We even inherited memories of the old Kanuga Club before Episcopalians from our parents, each of whom had had a brief encounter with that F. Scott Fitzgerald-glow of the sporting crowd at the old Inn. Mother, still wearing middy blouses, remembered the dances; Daddy described the blasé and glamorously hung-over young people that he could tell were "too fast" for him.

Sometimes Nancy and I loftily anoint ourselves guardians of the True Kanuga Spirit.

History of Kanuga? What could this Jack Reak know of those long-lost summer days in the '30s, of the white pine-spicy air, the magic lilt of Artie Shaw's *Stardust* or Tommy Dorsey's *Song of India* floating from the pavilion, that soft-brushed morning light and the blue-green afternoon shadows that are Kanuga.

Or of Rufus Morgan's dahlia garden and its hallelujah chorus of reds and pinks and yellows that poured forth sun-glory from the hot sticky crickety lake-edge flat that is now between the old and new tennis courts.

Nancy thought of the book parties at the old Pavilion when people dressed as characters out of literature and paraded in a circle to be judged. She was borne on Bishop Finlay's shoulders the night he was the Pied Piper, with a dozen other tots around his legs. The affair was rigged; the first place was the Pied Piper; the prize, already on hand, was a bag of suckers for all the children. The judge handed the bag to Nancy. Festivities were delayed so Nancy could be persuaded the whole bag of suckers did not belong just to her.

I wondered how he would describe those dark August thunderstorms that crashed over that old green-shingled Edwardian hotel, rain thrashing against the skylights of the rotunda, splaying water across the crazy geometry of the roof, splashing down the valleys like a continental river system, over-flowing gutters and downspouts and creating a chill, exciting world of make-believe danger.

And how will he describe the musty smell of the old pavilion, the smell of a warehouse of unbleached muslin; or convey the grace of the pavilion porch, deep and curved so artfully that couples drifting out from the dance floor at night hardly spoke, two cigarettes glowing in the dark, leaning on the wide railing looking out at the lake, as if they were on a luxury liner looking at the ocean.

Funny I should mention ocean liners.

After meeting Jack Reak at the slide-talk, Nancy and I were so impressed with his happy, direct manner, his unpretentious but precise intelligence, we insisted he sit with us at dinner that night. He was splendid company.

"What I'm doing is writing the history of an institution. It won't include the nostalgia," he said. He must have been reading our minds. This description of the book set me re-thinking my expectations.

But this re-thinking did not begin to prepare me for the dizzying shock to my perspective, not to say my ego, I got from reading the manuscript.

I felt like some dilettantish Henry James character aboard a great ocean liner who presumed to know the whims and moods of dear old *S.S. Majesty* from many crossings. But some sudden shock (iceberg?!) makes him realize how little he knows of the full reality.

He knows nothing of the engine room or the kitchen. He doesn't understand the first thing about navigation or how to deal with a storm at sea though he has chatted pleasantly with the ship's captain when invited to sit at his table. But he never asked about the steamship company that owns and operates the liner, or its board of directors and power struggles thereon, or banks and bankruptcy. Or the fierce driving vision of a few strong people needed to build it and keep it going.

That's a metaphor for the flash of insight about my knowledge of Kanuga I got from reading this book. And what I learned of the enormous effort it took, of the close calls with bankruptcy, of the piranha-like problems overcome, has made me see how little I, a guest period softie, ever knew about that other reality. My first reaction was to feel like a child stumbling on an adult secret— or Emily Webb in *Our Town*—and saying, "I never knew all that was going on." My second reaction was to love it more for knowing.

Rufus Morgan not only grew great dahlias, but as the book reveals, in that first shaky year of operations, 1928, he "became a legend for his ability to make every dollar count."

That first year Kanuga had a very shaky hold on survival. "Our first regular meal was a tragedy," one witness recalls. The next year's fare was described this way: "The food was fair now and then...mostly then, but somehow Messrs. Jackson and Finlay made people take it all as a sort of hilarious adventure...."

That's the kind of hustle it took time and again to keep alive this vision that started with the Rt. Rev. Kirkman George Finlay.

The book mentions book parties such as Nancy remembered but puts much more stress on the struggle to develop successful programs in pursuit of its central vision to further Christian life and education, Christian love and leadership.

Like all phases of today's success at Kanuga, program development experienced some crises of confidence. A program put on by Kanuga called "Science for Clergy" in 1969 was canceled for lack of interest while the 1970 "Impact of Science on Society" conference which brought distinguished public servants to Kanuga was not Kanuga sponsored.

I remember visiting Kanuga during the early days of the civil rights movement, wondering if my enchanted kingdom would ever catch on to the social revolution taking place around them.

Well, they did. After some early resistance, they were holding conferences on all kind of confrontational subjects with national black leaders like Vernon Jordan delivering keynote addresses. I remember being part of a Kanuga conference, along with Harry Golden, on the changing South.

I had a niece come back from a Young People's Conference quietly resolved never to be insensitive to other races.

Even my thunderstorms of "make-believe danger," was inappropriate romanticizing I learned from the book. The torrential rains of 1916 broke Kanuga's dam, (also the Toxaway dam, more famous in Southern folklore) which was rebuilt to make a much smaller lake. This was a major factor in the eventual decline in the Kanuga Club development. But the dam of the smaller Kanuga lake again gave way from the weight of heavy rains in 1928, the first year of the Episcopal Kanuga.

As for the old pavilion, I confess that, until I read this book, I had harbored a faint resentment that it had been torn down suddenly, without the notice such as was given to the end of the old hotel in 1967-68. But I learned from the book that this was an "act of God." An ice storm left it so wrecked, there was no choice but to let man finish the demolition.

This demolition opened a new dramatic view of the lake and led to the idea for the new pavilion to be designed with more see-through space. And few of us old sentimentalists would deny that the new one—which duly reflects the feeling of the old—is better suited for the location.

From this book I have learned that the original vision of Kanuga, as a religious conference center for the advancement of Christian life, has never wavered. Oh, there was one bishop who resigned from the staff at one point because he felt the work had become more commercial than pastoral. Also a generous contributor hurrumphed his resentment over the slick high-pressure fund-raising program that had been instituted and cut in half his usual contribution.

But if Kanuga had not gone to professional fund-raising it would not have been able to build the new hotel and conference center. Without that move, all of today's success would not have been possible.

The other thing that impressed me is the hard work the officials and members of the staff have always put into making it go. Some had more nerve than others. In 1967, for example, the board hesitated before signing on for the new building because all the fund-raising had not come through. As the book relates:

> Bishop Pinckney said that the board should sign the contract, "with faith and action, or to take the necessary steps to dissolve the corporation and sell the property."

While the fund-raising campaign was going into high gear, Mary Hartley described her day in the *Kanuga News:* "I would open the desk and greet the people and then run in the dining room and host there and then run to the canteen, and so on. It was like a Lucille Ball movie."

As for the smell of the old pavilion, it gets an epigraph to Chapter Five, written by Berkeley Grimball. It is a masterpiece of olfactory description. It does not tell of his scheme of bottling the smell to sell it to us old fools for $50 an ounce.

Now that I have read the book and recovered my equipoise, I realize that my poetries and memories are as much a part of the essential Kanuga as the struggles on the Board of Directors and the fund-raising. What I know and love may be just the outward, the beauty, but that is a visible part of God's blessing on Kanuga. This book simply reminds us that great enterprises for the glory of God survive, not only by faith and vision, but by hard work, shrewdness and a bit of hustle. How else were great cathedrals built or how were strong monasteries established? How else did Kanuga survive to be the blessed place it is today?

Joe Cumming
Carrollton, Georgia
October 1993

[Joseph B. Cumming, Jr., left the *Newsweek* magazine staff in 1979 after 22 years in the Atlanta news bureau. After gaining a master's degree at Emory University, he plunged into a teaching career in journalism and mass communication. His articles have appeared in national and regional publications and for four years he wrote a regular weekly column for the Sunday book section of the *Atlanta Journal Constitution.* Those who know Joe and his wife Emily know that five minutes after they arrive at Kanuga, he is already at work planning a skit or musical for presentation and recruiting other guests to help!]

Preface

"We are working hard to make this summer's program at Lake Kanuga a demonstration of the need of such a gathering place for our people," wrote the Rt. Rev. Kirkman George Finlay, May 25, 1928. It has been said that the word ka-nu-ga means "meeting place of many people" or "scratching place." These are interesting but not accurate uses of the word.

The Cherokee word ka-nu-ga (also written ca-nu-ga) has two meanings. It is an object and it is a place name. Kanuga is a tool—a scratching device used in the Cherokee vigorous ritual stick-ball game. One part of the ceremonial ritual was for the players to strip for scratching. The scratching then was done with a ka-nu-ga—a device resembling a short comb with seven teeth. The belief was that the scratching made the players tough and less liable to fall.

As a place name there was a Lower Cherokee settlement named ka-nu-ga, apparently on the waters of the Keowee River in South Carolina, destroyed in 1761. Also folklore places a traditional settlement by this name on the Pigeon River, in Haywood County, North Carolina. It was said to have been deserted before written history. It may have been located near the junction of the two forks of Pigeon River, a few miles east of present day Waynesville.

The Smithsonian linguist, John Harrington, in 1951, advised Kanuga's general manager Bill Verduin that the word Kanuga "evidently means 'scratching place.'" Modern Cherokee linguists do not concur. *The North Carolina Gazetteer* in 1968 carried an entry for "Kanuga Lake" which stated, "The Indian name traditionally meant 'The Meeting Place of Many Peoples.'" The writer provides no source or authority upon what such a translation was based.

When George Stephens began to build his Kanuga Lake Club in the early 1900s he accepted the folklore that Cherokee were said to have gathered at the flat rock, very close to Kanuga. It does seem reasonable to assume whoever was here would have enjoyed such a site. Whether Cherokee did ever gather on this part of their land which we call Kanuga we could know only by archeological diggings, including excavations under the lake.

We do know that since 1928, Episcopalians have been gathering at Kanuga. This book is an account of those gatherings. It is not a memorial book. It does not purport to list all the people who have contributed ever so much to make these gatherings possible and something special. It does not attempt to recall all the fun times or times of great inspiration these people together have shared. Rather, the author attempts to present a readable account of how the work begun by Kirkman Finlay has grown until Kanuga as an institution has continued to be a gathering place and at times a gathering place even for the representatives of the whole Anglican world—and for you and me.

Jack Reak
October 1993

The Cherokee symbols for ka-nu-ga are as follows:

ka—nu—ga

K A N U G A

Story of a Gathering Place

Chapter One
A Vision

We are planning to hold this summer two camps: one for men and boys, the other for women and girls. The purpose of both alike is the training and development of competent leaders in the work of the Church Schools and Young People's organizations. A place has been selected, the material and equipment is in sight, the leaders, in part at least, have been secured.[1]

The Rt. Rev. Kirkman George Finlay

The story that is to be Kanuga begins. The occasion is the first episcopal address to the annual convention of the new Diocese of Upper South Carolina, 1923. The speaker is the new bishop, Kirkman George Finlay. Until his election as bishop of the newly-formed diocese the previous year, he was bishop coadjutor of the Diocese of South Carolina and previous to that, he was rector of Trinity Church, Columbia. Immediately upon organization of the newly-created diocese, Finlay had established a Department of Religious Education with the immediate goal of establishing in each parish a Young People's Service League which would give an organizational structure to youth work throughout the diocese. The Spartanburg Church of the Advent rector, William Henry K. Pendleton, and Christ Church, Greenville, rector, Frank A. Juhan, would co-chair this work. Juhan immediately set about planning a summer camp like the one he had successfully conducted in Texas before coming to the Greenville church. This would be the pattern of activities that was to become Kanuga—people working together with a goodly supply of saints or heros, luck or divine intervention, much faith, and lots of hope.

The fledgling diocese held its first camp in the summer of 1923 at Woodside, property in Tigerville, South Carolina, lent them by William Thackston of Greenville. Rural Tigerville is about midpoint of a Greenville and Spartanburg, South Carolina, and a Flat Rock, North Carolina, triangle. The Young People's Service League camp was conducted for forty boys and then later a camp for forty girls followed. The campers used tents. There was no lake but the young boys during their camping session built a dam across a brook which the first rain washed away, one story from this time relates. Mr. Pendleton (Mr. was the clerical title in use at this time throughout the Carolinas) pronounced the endeavor a success.

It was indeed camping out. At the same time and not too far away, Presbyterian young people were enjoying the more considerable facilities of Montreat which had been since 1906 a conference and assembly center for the Presbyterian Church in the United States (South). In the same western North Carolina mountain area, the Southern Baptists in 1907 began building Ridgecrest. In 1908 the Methodist Episcopal Church South established their Lake Junaluska assembly and camping facility near Waynesville. Presbyterian, Baptist, and Methodist assembly grounds encouraged private cottage development as part of the family focus they incorporated into their purposes.

Those Upper South Carolina diocesan clergy who were pioneering a summer outdoor leadership development program were very much aware of what the other denominations were accomplishing and sought for their church similar facilities for denominational growth and leadership development. The five Carolina dioceses began participating together in 1924 in a Church Training School Conference conducted each year in July at the old Mission School at Valle Crucis, North Carolina. Participants were church school teachers, leaders of the women's auxiliary, and others active in parish life. Schools of this type were becoming increasingly important throughout the church for leadership training. But Valle Crucis was inaccessible for many South Carolina Episcopalians. They arrived either by bus (at $3.50) or by train to Lenoir and then disembarked for a bus ride up to the Mission School property. The cost of the full twelve-day conference was $20. The Valle Crucis conferences did, however, continue there until 1928 when they were moved to Kanuga.

The second annual convention of the Diocese of Upper South Carolina was held in January 1924, at the Church of the Advent in Spartanburg. The Young People's Service League provided focus for the diocesan youth program and had become a network for interest in the summer camp idea. By the time of the second convention there were fifteen functioning youth groups in the separate parishes. In his address to the convention the bishop said that the past summer's camps "were most successful from every angle." And in considerable detail Bishop Finlay set forth his vision for a needed conference center:

> *Last spring I spoke to you of a summer conference. I can now speak of it as an accomplished fact.... I can hardly speak too highly of the splendid work done by those who planned and carried out the program* [The Rev. Frank A. Juhan, The Rev. W. H. K. Pendleton, and The Rev. W. P. Peyton].... *William Thackston of Greenville turned over to us his splendid camp and equipment. Mrs. Frank N. Callen led the Conferences of the Girls' Camp in a thoroughly efficient and practical way....*
>
> *We have seen what can be accomplished by a few days spent together in work and play and fellowship. Now we are asking, why not a Camp of Church School Workers, of Lay-readers, of the Clergy themselves? Why not a meeting of our Vestrymen similar to the one held recently in Columbia, but lasting for a longer period, and giving opportunity for more thorough discussion and closer fellowship? And, last but not least, why not a summer colony growing up around the Conference Grounds such as has become such an essential feature in the work of our sister Churches at Montreat, Bon Clarken, and Junaluska?*
>
> *Now three [sic] North Carolina dioceses are, at least, interested in cooperating with us in such a plan....*
>
> *A very remarkable proposition has been made us which will be brought to your attention later. By it, we would be put at once, in the matter of equipment, where our brethren of the other churches are after years of labor.*[2]

Some time in the fall of 1923, George Stephens, president and principal stockholder of the Kanuga Lake Inn near Hendersonville, North Carolina, let it be known that the property was for sale and was particularly suitable for a church conference center which implied special financial considerations. The summer hotel which began as a private club in 1909 with cottages, lake and golf course, carriage house and stables, had prospered only in its early years and was now on the financial rocks. Bishop

Finlay shared this news with Mr. Pendleton who wrote: "From that day for many years I was to work at Bishop Finlay's side through ups and downs—and they were mainly downs—in the struggle for Kanuga. Our people wanted something good, but Kanuga seemed to many too great to be more than an idle dream."[3]

A resolution was placed before the Upper South Carolina diocesan convention from the delegates who had attended the Province of Sewanee meeting earlier that year and had there discussed conference center needs. At the Chattanooga meeting the Upper South Carolina diocesan delegates adopted a resolution requesting the bishops of the dioceses in the two Carolinas and the bishops of the dioceses of Atlanta and Georgia to appoint a committee to investigate and report to their respective diocesan authorities "with regard to the location of a permanent Summer Conference and Assembly Ground for the benefit of their Dioceses and others that might wish to join them."

Such a committee was appointed and "after making a thorough investigation" reported that the Hendersonville Kanuga Lake property was the unanimous choice for a "Summer Conference and Assembly Ground for the Episcopalians of the Southeast." Somehow a report of this group's activities got to the press and several papers reported that the Episcopal church was going to spend $360,000 to build conference facilities in Western North Carolina.

The authority to act on the motion came in an amended resolution which read: "That the Executive Council appoint a committee of five, to be composed of the Bishop, two clergymen, and two laymen, to go thoroughly into the Kanuga Lake proposition...and report to the Executive Council of this Diocese."

In the meantime, the next summer (1924) was coming and plans were under way for a second diocesan-sponsored camp. They would work with what they had. Mr. Juhan rented the North Carolina Bowman's Bluff property of A. W. Smith of Greenville for a camp site. The property was located near the French Broad River and near Etowah. A small Episcopal church, Gethsemane, built in 1886 to serve primarily families of British heritage who had come to this area, had made the area popular with summer area visitors who were Episcopalians.

And the second summer camp was successful. The diocesan report called Juhan's leadership inspiring and stated that nearly

170 young people "with their Councillors [sic] and Leaders spent two wonderful weeks in camp.... Practically the whole morning was given to instruction and inspirational service. The afternoon and evening were kept free for recreation. Firm but kindly discipline was maintained with military precision." The price was $1.00 a day, the total expenses were $1,919, and the camp's financial ledger registered $55.25 above expenses.

Immediately following the young people's camp was scheduled a training conference for diocesan parish workers. There was an attendance of about fifty extending to seventy for part of the session. This conference was acknowledged to have been hastily put together, and the two courses, "The Pupil" and "Principles of Christian Nurture," were courses required for credits toward entrance into the Nationally Accredited Teachers Association. Sponsored by the national church's Department of Religious Instruction, these formal study courses were popular self-improvement classes for church-school teachers. Grades were printed in the diocesan convention proceedings. The total expenses were $559.79, and receipts were $388.14, leaving a manageable deficit of $171.65.

Beginning with the summer of 1925, the Diocese of Upper South Carolina and the Diocese of South Carolina together rented the property of Camp Transylvania (today the Brevard Music Center property) just outside Brevard, North Carolina, for the Young People's Conferences. This summer camp was named Ellison Capers and honored the Confederate general who later became a bishop and who had maintained a summer residence in nearby Cedar Mountain. Bishop Finlay was camp director. The Rev. H. W. Starr was dean of faculty and the Rev. W. H. K. Pendleton was chaplain.

Beginning also with the summer of 1925, a second camping site entered the picture. On August 11, 1925, Bishop Finlay, Mr. Pendleton, and D. E. McCuen, acting on behalf of the diocese, purchased for five dollars from Dr. Stephen Brown of Hendersonville, 200 acres of land at See Off located between Cedar Mountain and Brevard.[4] The property is just off the old Greenville Highway (NC #276). The See Off land gift would provide Bishop Finlay with enough land so that he could begin to organize and to build his proposed assembly ground. The new land holders agreed to some legal encumbrances: improvements of $1,000 were required of a permanent nature although good faith delays were negotiable; a dam and lake could be built; additional land could in time be acquired; and property could be sold to other Episcopalians for cottage construction. The property would revert to the owner if the terms of the sale were not met, indicating that the $5.00 sale price was indeed a gift from Dr. Brown who wanted to help the Bishop in his endeavor to secure a permanent conference center. Brown, a prominent Hendersonville physician who was active in religious, fraternal, and civic affairs, had been a member of the Kanuga Lake Club since its incorporation. He knew there was little likelihood of success for the few who were still interested in securing the Kanuga property for a conference center. The considerable cost was simply beyond foreseeable means. The acquisition of this See Off mountain property at this time was a major decision reconciling Bishop Finlay's realism on how a needed conference center was going to have to come about. They simply would have to do it the hard way—begin and build from scratch.

The first person to use the See Off property was the Rev. A. Rufus Morgan of Columbia, South Carolina, who this same summer had taken a group of junior boys up to the new camp site for what surely was a rugged adventure.[5]

Concurrently with the acquisition of this See Off land, the diocesan committee appointed to investigate the possibility of acquiring Kanuga Lake property was continuing its slow and unsuccessful work in arousing interest wide enough for the idea to have financial viability. There was, in fact, little interest other than among a few in the Upper South Carolina diocese, chiefly Rufus Morgan and William Pendleton. From its inception in 1924, the commission had taken seriously its charge to study possibilities. In November 1924, they traveled over unpaved roads visiting every site offered in the mountain region they had selected. A room-by-room inventory of the Kanuga property was made. Hotel men were consulted about expenses of operation and sources of income, and two appraisals were made and the value of Kanuga was placed at or near $300,000. The report to the diocesan convention in 1925 stated that because the advantages of Kanuga so far surpassed those of any other property offered they did not consider it necessary to report in detail except with regard to that property. The report was rejected as unrealistic. The last act of Mr.

Juhan in the diocese was to vote in favor of the resolution in the committee. He was consecrated bishop of Florida in November 1925, bringing to an end his work with the committee. It seemed like a prophetic conclusion to the Kanuga Lake property hope.

Summers and summer camps came in 1926 and 1927 and camp statistics document real growth of the joint South Carolina and North Carolina summer camping activities. The Brevard rental facilities were satisfactory and Camp Ellison Capers was administered by a committee representing the cooperating dioceses which selected a camp director.[6] Bishop Finlay had no rivals for the job.

Morehouse Publishing Company's 1931, *Believing Youth: A Cheering Experience in Creative Teaching,* is an account by author Homer W. Starr of his experimental teaching at Camp Capers. Starr had been chaplain of Porter Military Academy in Charleston and Chapel of the Cross rector and student pastor at the University of North Carolina, Chapel Hill, before being asked to teach at the summer camp. The book was favorably reviewed by the leading religious journals the same year it was published. The author's 1931 preface reflected his enthusiasm:

> *In the summer of 1925 I was asked to teach a course on "Personal Religion" at Camp Ellison Capers, which that year was attended by something over two hundred young people from North and South Carolina. It was not known how many of them would be interested in such a subject, and I was in some doubts as to the best method of teaching it. I finally decided to make a bold experiment in creative teaching, and instead of preparing a set of lectures on self-chosen topics, to allow the members of the class to construct their own course from day to day by means of their questions, and to present no subject for their consideration which was not suggested by themselves. The results of this experiment were such as to lead me to repeat it every year since that time at Camp Ellison Capers, Valle Crucis, N.C., Lake Kanuga, N.C., and the Young People's Conference of the Summer Training School at Sewanee, Tennessee.*[7]

Bishop Finlay's interest in the new See Off camp site is evident from his recorded activities. He records May 10–15 (1926) spending a week with clergy and laymen, "constructing the first unit of our summer camp development. This shack 34 x 16 ft. will be used for the boys' camp this summer.... The camp will run at the same time as Camp Ellison Capers, June 18–July 1."

The bishop's log for June 18–July 1 the same year records his visit to Camp Ellison Capers (Camp Transylvania) where there was an attendance of 210. "One of the most enjoyable occasions was the hike to See Off, our wonderful piece of property near Brevard."

In 1926 the camps enrolled over 200 and the 1927 camp enrolled 160. The See Off 1926 camp was for younger boys only and the 1927 See Off camping session held a camp for 14 girls in addition to its boys' camp. Bishop Finlay with Mr. Morgan's assistance directed both. Several women assisted him with the girls' camping activities. The property now had "one sleeping shack" which could accommodate 18 to 20, and the other a combined kitchen and dining room with a capacity of about 26. That summer they began work on a chapel.

James Morrow of Brevard, whose father built camps in Transylvania County, recalls visiting the camp site after Bishop Finlay moved his activities to Kanuga. The See Off land lay idle for some time. Morrow remembers the buildings as saw-mill shacks typical of camping accommodations erected in the area at that time—simple half-walled frame buildings with screen wire extending all around the upper half of the buildings. Since during the short time Bishop Finlay used the camp site, he did not conform to the covenants and restrictions on the title, the property reverted to the original owner. Today only a broken stone foundation remains of that venture.

Chapter Two
Dream to Reality

This magnificent property will then belong to the Church. What its possession as a training ground for our young people and adults and as a place for various groups will mean is hard to over-estimate.[1]

Bishop Kirkman Finlay

Bishop Finlay's November 1928 address to his diocese in convention asserts that a dream is becoming a reality. This Kanuga Lake property is a story in itself. To understand Kanuga is to understand just how it came into being and the romance held for this property by so many. And like the Kanuga story in general, this is a story about people.

George Erwin Cullet Stephens was born April 8, 1873, in Guilford County, North Carolina. A football scholarship plus his knowledge of stenography provided the means for him to work his way through the University of North Carolina at Chapel Hill. He settled in Charlotte in 1896, the year he was graduated from the University. Sports fans would be interested to know that Stephens, who was one of Chapel Hill's most celebrated athletes, also is credited with catching the first forward pass in football. He remained in Charlotte until 1921, when for reasons of his family's health he moved to Asheville. Stephens began his career in the Charlotte insurance firm of Brem, Stephens, and Brem. In 1902, with his Winston-Salem boyhood banking friend, Word H. Wood, he joined F. C. Abbott in organizing the Southern States Trust Company. The name later was changed to the American Trust Company which was the predecessor of the North Carolina National Bank. Through a series of mergers, it has become

NationsBank. In 1912 Stephens and Wood purchased an interest in *The Charlotte Observer* and later became the paper's sole owners.[2]

Stephens' energies were apparently limitless. He was a director of the company (bearing his name) which he organized in Charlotte in 1910 to develop an elite suburban enclave known as Myers Park, which his company developed under the comprehensive landscape plan of John Nolen, one of the nation's foremost city-planning authorities. The 1,200-acre tract had been a cotton plantation of his father-in-law, John S. Myers, and Myers Park attracted national attention as one of the South's leading examples of a planned residential development. Nolen employed the talents of some of the better-known municipal architects of the nation.

While engaged in his Myers Park real estate development, Stephens was also buying 1,500 acres of property in pursuance of another idea. The essence of the idea was the cooperative spirit as applied to the high cost of summer living in a second home. By allowing one business management to supply their wants, those who chose to go away for the summers could greatly decrease their costs of living and at the same time provide the quality of summer family recreation and congeniality which "gentlemen of modest fortune or income" would desire. He investigated a number of such clubs, several in the Adirondacks, one in New York, and one in Wisconsin. He felt certain that the same thing could be accomplished on a smaller scale by and for like kindred responsible Southern men in the Blue Ridge Mountains of North Carolina. He laid the plan before seventy-five or more practical business acquaintances who gave their support.

In 1898, Stephens had begun annual summer visits to Western North Carolina where he had purchased a summer home in Flat Rock. A wonderful story explains Stephens' introduction to the Flat Rock area. The story is told by Scotty Robertson who was an early Kanuga staff member and later organist of St. James Episcopal Church in Wilmington, North Carolina:

> *George Stephens told me once that if he had not missed a train by about two minutes, probably there would not have been a Kanuga. Back in those days one came to Hendersonville from Asheville by Southern Railway. One day Mr. Stephens went to the depot to catch the midday train to Asheville.... When he*

arrived he saw the train disappearing down the track. A Hendersonville real estate man asked him what he was going to do with himself until the afternoon train came along. Mr. Stephens said he had nothing to do. The agent invited him to get in his buggy and ride out to look at some choice property about six miles out of town.... He bought it.[3]

Stephens' Kanuga Lake Club, a gigantic cooperative summer residential colony in the western mountains of North Carolina, was one of Stephens' crowning achievements. The plan was first publicly announced in 1908.[4] The colony was to be located on the old Hanckel property near Hendersonville and Flat Rock. A ten-year club membership would cost $150 payable in $15 monthly installments. The money derived from the first two hundred members—$30,000—would be used for the capital development of the property. Stephens' profit would come from the appreciation that lakefront lots would incur after the club had been in successful operation over a few years. Only the first 200 members would enjoy the initial bargain prices. The plan would accommodate from 700 to 1,000 members. *The Charleston Evening Post* in July 29, 1910, stated that "up till now George Stephens has spent $155,000 on the work." Stephens was the sole owner and the expected capital outlay was thought to be more than $200,000.

A 100-acre lake would be the central feature of the landscape design. Its topography marked the lake and surrounding accessible land as a natural amphitheatre walled around by mountains which could be seen range on range. The lake would be formed by a substantial dam across a stream that flows into Mud Creek which in turn is a tributary of the French Broad River. It would provide a very large lake with about four miles of roadway around it affording lake view and lake-accessible lots. The development was scheduled to open July 1 for the 1909 summer season.

A second feature of the colony was a large clubhouse which would be essentially a high-class summer hotel, a kind of residential accommodation becoming increasingly popular and financially successful at this time throughout the western mountains of North Carolina. The privilege of membership accorded residence in the clubhouse at actual cost—$8 per week for adults and $4 for children—or one could live in one of the modern cottages that were to be built and take meals at the clubhouse. Tennis courts, baseball grounds, golf links, drives, and bridle paths completed this family-oriented resort. There would be no alcoholic beverages in any of the public facilities.

Membership was limited to those personally known by Stephens or recommended by some member of the colony as memberships grew. Stephens, who also was a trustee of the University of North Carolina (his special love and where he had served as a trustee of that institution since about five years after his graduation), relied on his circle of friends at Chapel Hill and his Charlotte Myers Park friends for his initial clientele of kindred kind. Chapel Hill president, Francis Preston Venable, was one of the first to enroll and Dr. C. S. Mangum of the University would be the resident physician. Others followed because they too liked the idea. A kindergarten and a "boys' leader" were built into the plan. Family accommodations without the domestic problems of cooking and organized activities for all were a portfolio that Stephen envisioned in the mountains to equal the success he had enjoyed with his Myers Park development in Charlotte.

To each of the first 200 members of the colony, a 200 x 50 foot lot was given and an attractive six-room house would be built on this lot for the member at $1,000—the actual cost. There was no desire to make any profit on any building for the membership. Each cottage would have a telephone and electric lights. Electricity would be generated from the falls below the dam on the property. Water for the clubhouse and for the cottages would come from high up in the mountains. No cottage costing less than $400 or more than $2,500 was permitted. Horses could be boarded for a fee.

Kanuga, from the first announcement of intent, attracted the attention of the architectural and planning community of the nation because of two individuals Stephens had selected to put it all together—John Nolen and Richard Sharp Smith. Nolen (after the death in 1903 of Frederick Law Olmsted) ranked at the top of American designers and planners in the new twentieth century. Nolen's Boston-based company had prepared the notable plan for Myers Park at the invitation of Stephens. In 1908 he was at the dawn of a career that would encompass 400 commissions nationwide and a leading role in the founding of the American City Planning Institute. His bibliography in *Who's Who in America* (1926-27) identifies a laundry list of important assignments including the 1926 master plan for the city of Asheville. The book,

Early Twentieth-Century Suburbs of North Carolina, has a photograph of Nolen and the caption under the picture lists both Kanuga Lake Resort and an expansion of the campus of the University of North Carolina at Chapel Hill as his accomplishments.[5]

The architect Richard Sharp Smith had a long and distinguished Asheville architecture and building practice. Smith came to Asheville to work on the Biltmore House and remained to found his own practice. Smith designed the Asheville Young Men's Institute building which Vanderbilt gave to the city's black citizens in 1892. He worked continuously in Asheville for almost thirty years with the bulk of his commissions from 1900 to 1915. Smith designed in a wide range of styles, often with much originality as in his Asheville Montford neighborhood homes which include the popular shingle style such as he used in the Kanuga property designs. Smith also was the architect of St. Mary's and Grace Episcopal churches in Asheville. Smith was the architect of the second part of In the Oaks, the Franklin Silas Terry mansion at Black Mountain, North Carolina.[6]

At Kanuga Lake, George Stephens could take pride in the success of his venture. Kanuga Lake Club opened in 1909 as advertised. The clubhouse with its oak interior was in operation and twelve cottages had been built. Still in progress at the time of opening was the nine-hole golf course that crisscrossed a road that later was named Crab Creek Road and then even later Kanuga Road. In October 1909, problems developed with the dam and it was necessary to empty the lake and make costly repairs to it.

In late summer, 1910, a furniture shop under the supervision of Rufus Franklin Huneycutt was opened where "mission style" furniture was made from Kanuga wood and used at the club or sold through stores. The furniture was similar to the craftsmanship of the young American Gustav Stickley which was enjoying wide popularity at the turn of the century. Stephens planned for the shop to conduct a small manual-training school operation providing mountain boys an opportunity to learn a useful trade in conjunction with the sales of these manufactured pieces. The shop made much of the furniture used in the Kanuga Club. Furniture from the shop at that time was avant-garde and was shipped throughout the Southeast and occasionally can still be found in antique shops. The shop remained in operation until the flood of 1916.

A brochure for the 1911 season listed many "permanent improvements since last year: the pavilion and the boat house, a new billiard room, a larger children's dining room, a new telephone line to Hendersonville, a Western Union telegraph office, an ice and refrigerating plant, and improved accommodations for servants." It was noted that the golf links were greatly improved with new grass and noted was the removal of stumps and stones. Regatta week, golf week, music week, tennis week, and dramatic week were all arranged by club committee members. The baseball team was complete with uniforms.

A *Charleston Daily Observer* reporter wrote about the closing days of the fourth social season at Kanuga: "The popular resort will close September 20, but its fame is far-reaching." The accomplishments of the many young people were noted. The "delightful golf party" was described and the "Alumni Council of the University of North Carolina" was entertained. Col. P. H. Nelson, who was identified "as one of the most distinguished lawyers in the Palmetto State" and "his charming wife" were frequently described as the most popular couple at the club. A folio of pictures depicts a happy lot of children and adults in a Victorian-staged setting with the caption: "Grown-ups often share the pleasures with the children at Kanuga." The photograph is of a drop-the-handkerchief party in progress.

The 1913 brochure mentioned that while the club was patronized primarily by members, in the past four years non-members had been allowed. The club facilities were compared to those "usual to high-class mountain-lake resorts," but noted that Kanuga was meant to be "free from many of [their] extravagancies and artificialities." Club members were called "Kanugans" or "Tribesmen" as a promotional effort and to strengthen the community bond which Stephens and other members sincerely sought in this unique cooperative endeavor. Stephens engaged the Wood and Harvey hotel chain for the management of the club. The successful firm also at this time managed the Hampton Terrace of Augusta and the fashionable Toxaway Inn at nearby Lake Toxaway.

The only record from 1914 is a July 23, 1914, daily report from the operating department of the club which noted 83 adult guests, 37 children, 31 servants, and no visitors. No records of

1915 exist, but 1916 almost brought an end to the club that Stephens had instituted "where there are no flaming advertisements on the walls, where there is no clerk with a diamond in his shirt and no running to and fro of flunkies after the tips that they live for...a hotel that is not a hotel because it is a club."

Rain. For ten days it rained! It began the night of July 3, 1916. It was supposed to stop for the holiday, but it did not. It cleared for a couple of days and then it began again. It rained ten inches July 15 and 16. At 2:00 a.m. Sunday, July 16, in the black of darkness, "the Kanuga Lake dam gave way and with a mighty roar the waters of Henderson County's largest dam poured forth," was the way one reporter described the event. Later that morning, two other county dams broke—Osceola Lake dam and at about the same hour, the Jordan Mill dam. Hendersonville was awash in water and mud. By Sunday afternoon the railroad bed and trestles south of Hendersonville were washed away as far down the line as Tryon.

In Asheville, the flooding was severe. Pictures of the high water in the streets of the mountain city seem almost unbelievable today. In adjoining Transylvania County, the 50-foot-high dam at Lake Toxaway broke. The luxury hotel there was dependent on the lake and did not recover. Kanuga, too, was in many ways dependent on its lake both aesthetically and for recreation.

The Kanuga dam was rebuilt, but smaller, and the lake was one-fourth the size it had been. There were rumors that the club was losing popularity with its members. The local newspaper, *The French Broad Hustler,* reported in the fall of 1916: "By far the best news that has come from Kanuga in a long time is the announcement that they are going to have an 18-hole golf course."[7] Stephens wrote a letter to the editor of the Hendersonville paper in anticipation of the 1918 summer season lamenting that Kanuga was rarely mentioned in his paper. He stated that the outlook for the coming season was bright and called attention to the fact that Kanuga Club had been the means of locating investments in Henderson County in the aggregate of over one-half-million dollars. Kanuga had the first sand-clay road in North Carolina, he told them.

The grand cooperative colony was all over in February 1919, when papers were filed for the incorporation of a new company, The Kanuga Club. Capital stock assets were listed at $150,000, divided into fifteen hundred shares at the par value of one hundred dollars per share and the corporation was authorized to commence business with a capital stock of three hundred dollars. Stephens would try to sell shares at a low speculative price.

George Stephens tried for a few years to make his Kanuga Club competitive in the summer tourist industry. The Hendersonville weekly newspaper in the early 1920s printed a "Round the Hotels—With Our Summer Visitors" page. Kanuga Lake Inn, the name still used in publicity, ran advertisements in competition for business with other summer tourist hotels. Three-bedroom cottages rented for $200 for the season and adults paid $17.50 board for a week. Rooms at the Inn were $8.00 per week. The orchestra continued to play at the lakeshore, there was a bit of genteel gambling at the gaming tables, and from time to time, noted entertainers performed at the club.

A land boom the oldtimers still talk about hit its peak in Hendersonville and Henderson County in 1925 and 1926. There was another Kanuga reorganization. This venture was named Kanuga, Incorporated. The capital stock was listed at $100,000 and again with a par value of one hundred dollars, the corporation would begin business when $20,000 composed of 200 shares were subscribed for. This did not sell. Kanuga Estates, Incorporated, was organized in September 1925. For this attempt to cash in on the land boom, Stephens enlisted as directors two West Palm Beach, Florida, residents along with H. Walter Fuller, a Hendersonville resident who was in charge of the publicity for Laurel Park Estates in the same county.[8] The capital stock was listed this time as $300,000 consisting of 3,000 shares at a par value of one hundred dollars.

The property did not sell even in this period of land speculation. Kanuga had been designed for another day. The war and the automobile had made obsolescent the reasons the Kanuga colony had been formed. When Kanuga was built, the "summer people" came to the mountains by train. They brought trunks and many of them stayed all summer to avoid the heat. By the late 1920s, however, people were no longer staying all summer at Kanuga. Automobiles had become quite commonplace and people did not "go and stay" as they once did. In 1910 there were 400,000 automobiles in the United States; in 1918 there were 3,500,000. World War I doomed Stephens' idea of social class togetherness especially in the university world which Stephens had very much depended on to buy into his venture of institutionalizing social distance. The decline of Kanuga expectations was evident even by 1916 when the dam was replaced in a way that considerably reduced the lake to its present size.

Stephens' initial Kanuga sale offer to Bishop Finlay was made when he first learned that some of the Episcopal dioceses might be interested in purchasing the property. He made an offer to sell the property for $186,000—the whole property, containing 900 acres with a lake of about 24 acres, 39 cottages, clubhouse, four annexes, garage, livery stable, and servants' quarters. Bishop Finlay wrote that he spent quite a bit of time trying to find support from about thirteen other Southeastern dioceses for the offer and found only one or two interested. That offer he realistically did not then pursue further.

Stephens then, in the winter of 1927-28, made an offer to Bishop Finlay of 400 acres, including the lake and all buildings, for $95,000. This offer was a realistic appraisal on the part of real estate-knowledgeable Stephens that Kanuga was now suited for only a large membership association group and that his own Episcopal church was probably the most likely. Stephens said that he would undertake to raise the amount himself if the bishops of the five Carolina dioceses expressed their desire to own the property. All five bishops gave him letters of endorsement.

With headquarters in Asheville, an organization of laymen was formed to put together the money for the Kanuga purchase. The goal was to raise at least $100,000, buy Kanuga, and turn it over to a church board of trustees. The executive committee consisted of Judge Michael Schenck, of Hendersonville, chairman; Asheville resident Harry M. Roberts, vice-chairman; F. Roger Miller, secretary; Walter P. Taylor, treasurer; W. Vance Brown, George Stephens, and Harry W. Love, directors; and Dr. W. R. Kirk of Hendersonville, director. An advisory committee of W. A. Erwin of Durham, George B. Elliott of Wilmington, O. T. Waring of Charleston, and Christie Benet of Columbia, extended participation throughout the two Carolinas.

Stephens, assisted by Harry Love, developed literature and began to solicit funds. The committee decided that fund-raising would be easier if Kanuga could show a successful season as an Episcopal center and accordingly Stephens loaned the property to the Diocese of Upper South Carolina for the summer of 1928. The proposed property purchase was described in this way:

> *400 acres...small artificial lake on the shores of which is Kanuga Village...about 50 buildings...of a rambling, roomy type, the main building and four annexes connected to it under one roof contain 125 bedrooms...the dining room has a seating capacity of 500...a private dining room which seats 20, and another medium-sized dining room that will seat 150...everything is electrically lighted...39 cottages from 3 to 7 rooms each...on the shore of the lake immediately in front of the main building is a large pavilion having an auditorium 50 x 100 feet with stage...below the auditorium and under a portion of the building which extends out over the lake are dressing rooms for bathers....*

Raising money to buy Kanuga was a trying business. Stephens himself headed the list of contributors with $5,000. One cannot ask others to give without being deeply involved oneself, the professional money-raiser knew. They reached about $45,000 and things stopped. "We visited every gathering of Episcopalians...where we could speak or use any influence for Kanuga. We endeavored in every way to keep the movement alive and gain friends for it," Mr. Pendleton wrote expressing his dogged determination that Kanuga should be a reality. Pendleton had been rector of Spartanburg's Church of the Advent since 1909, and had been chairman of the Department of Religious Education in the Diocese of Upper South Carolina since the diocese was formed in 1922. He never wavered in his determination that Kanuga should belong to the church even when the asking price seemed impossible to achieve. Later, in March 1928, serious illness prevented him from any work for two years. His Spartanburg Church of the Advent followed through, however, with a $12,000 contribution which he had been working to secure.

Bishop Finlay made two trips to New York to solicit funds. He raised $600 the first trip, with $500 coming from a Presbyterian. George Stephens then went to New York to talk with some influential men he knew and opened the way for a second visit by Bishop Finlay. Finlay wrote of that second New York venture:

> *I was told a luncheon would be given by three men and I would be the speaker. When I arrived in New York, two of the men had backed out, but the third said he would host the luncheon if I would be responsible for the guest list. With the help of the Rev.*

Nathan A. Seagle, I worked up a list of 30 leading Episcopalians in New York, most of them with a Southern connection. I wrote them personal invitations to the luncheon. Some of them wrote that they could not come, others ignored the invitation altogether. On the day of the luncheon, not even the host attended.

A Pennsylvania speaking engagement arranged by a friend in the area netted between $300 and $400. When he returned home, the Bishop received a letter from the Pennsylvania layman friend with a contribution of $15,000 and then a few days later, from the same friend, a check for $5,500. The campaign still was about $30,000 short of its goal which now necessarily had been raised to $104,000 because of back taxes and expenses. There were no other apparent sources of income left.

Bishop Finlay again contacted his Pennsylvania friend, but this time asking for a loan. He received a $25,000 gift. The donor wanted to remain anonymous and only years later did it become known that Alan Wood of Bryn Mawr was Kanuga's enabling benefactor. Wood, at the time of the gift, was the major shareholder of Alan Wood Steel Company of Conshohocken, Pennsylvania. His introduction to the Carolinas was by way of a Charleston marriage. The Woods had a summer home in Flat Rock and became friends of the Finlays when they were at St. John-in-the-Wilderness Church, Flat Rock, during the summers.

Thus, the new management came into possession of the Kanuga property free of all legal obligations in the way of old debts or mortgages. The only claim was the remaining $8,500 which was underwritten by the owners (by Stephens as principal stockholder) and by Bishop Finlay. The bishop borrowed his money from equity in his private insurance policies.

A problem for the future was recognized at the time the property sale was made final. Bishop Finlay had secured title to only 400 acres of the 950-acre parcel that really was needed to have a coherent conference site. While the new owners had a lake, the boundary line ran through the center of the dam.

The property was turned over to the Dioceses of Upper South Carolina, South Carolina, East North Carolina, and Western North Carolina. The Diocese of North Carolina declined to participate, for the reason, as reported by its executive council, "That this Diocese was financially unable to assume the necessary obligations for the ownership and operation of the property." In 1929, a committee of laymen was appointed to reconsider the proposal. This committee reported unfavorably, and the executive council again declined to recommend becoming part of Kanuga Conferences.

The Kanuga property legally would be held by a holding body of one trustee from each diocese with a governing Board of Managers consisting of the bishops, one clergyman, one layman, the president of the Woman's Auxiliary, and one young person from each diocese. Bishop Finlay's ideas about real youth involvement were ahead of his time. However, young people did not get representation because of the serious reservation of one bishop who questioned their general maturity to make decisions of the kind board membership would entail. The constitution of the new corporation was adopted October 11, 1929, and the official name was Kanuga Conferences Association.[9]

1. George Erwin Cullet Stephens
   1873–1946
   Wilford S. Conrow, 1943 portrait of George Stephens.
   (Photograph courtesy: Mint Museum of Art, Charlotte, North Carolina)

2. Exterior view of corridor to Kanuga Lake Club Inn Annex sleeping accommodations.

3. Interior view of same corridor.

4.   Kanuga Lake Club Inn with "mission style" oak chairs and tables which are still in use.

5.   Kanuga Lake Club Inn lobby.

6. Sleeping cottages design was three connecting sleeping rooms and a long hall with the end of hall curtained off for servant's cot when desired. (circa 1909)

7. Drop-the-handkerchief game in progress was popularly portrayed to convey idea of Kanuga Lake Club as a family resort.

8.   Pavilion
(Photograph courtesy Baker-Barber Collection, Hendersonville)

9.   Pavilion
Lake Kanuga with Pinnacle Mountain in the background.
(Photograph courtesy Baker-Barber Collection, Hendersonville)

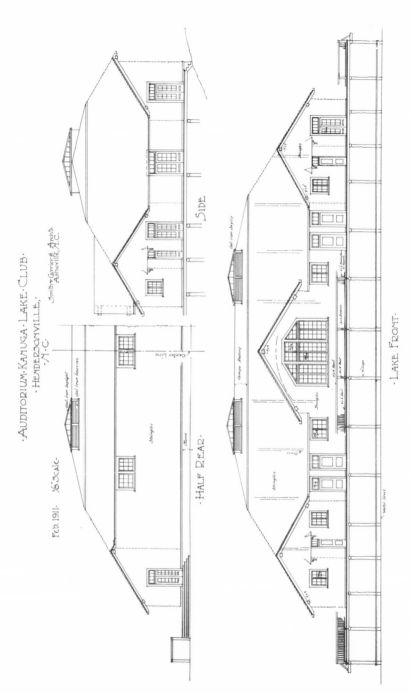

10. Richard Sharp Smith original 1911 architectural pavilion drawing.
    (Photoprint courtesy Historical Resources Commission of Asheville and Buncombe County, North Carolina)

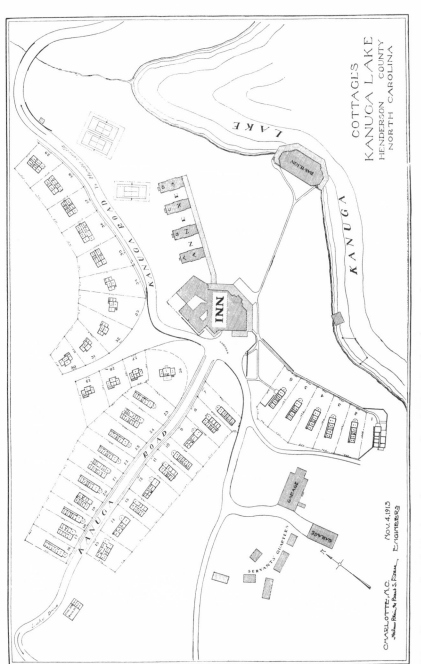

11. Engineer's 1913 plat of proposed cottage site development.

12. kanuga
    (Photograph
    courtesy
    Museum of the
    Cherokee
    Indian,
    Cherokee,
    North Carolina)

Chapter Three
Early Years

I learned to know and appreciate his simple faith and sublime courage and nobility of spirit. Because he saw a vision of a great training ground for the youth of the Carolinas, he allowed no doubts or fears or lack of material resources to hold him back. We can say with all truth that Kanuga was made a splendid reality because of the faith and high courage of Kirkman Finlay.[1]

The Rt. Rev. Albert S. Thomas

"That was a memorable season (1928).... None of us knew anything about running a hotel or even a conference on a large scale. We made our preliminary arrangements, set up our faculty, our kitchen staff, and opened. We found we were under-manned, under-staffed and under-equipped at almost every point. Our first regular meal was a tragedy," a participant years later wrote. And the meal was an hour late too.[2]

Food, shelter, worship, and recreation are the ingredients of camp life. "Imagine the amazing inexperience of the dear soul who volunteered to do the cooking, when we found her fluttering around the stove the first morning trying to poach eggs for 185 howling, hungry, teen-agers!" another account of that trial first year reports.

Realizing their deficiencies in the food-preparation domain, they increased the kitchen staff and put one person in charge of management—Walter Taylor, who had come to the camp to build some needed new boats since the old ones were rotting and unsafe. "The food was fair now and then, mostly then, but somehow Messrs. Jackson and Finlay made people take it all as a sort of hilarious adventure," said one who was there. That same reporter said: "The beds were like hammocks, hot water in the bathroom was infrequent and in the far cottages, an illusion." Bishop Finlay who planned the meals also lost ten pounds the first week.

Boys at the junior camp, officially ages 12-14 years but with some younger, were housed in old World War I army tents located at what now is the Wildlife Camp. The boys joined the girls for meals, programs, and swimming. Volleyball was popular as well as relay races. There was a fancy dress dance one night during camp. All campers were advised that the tenting could be cold and to bring at least two blankets. Eleven-year-old William Jones Gordon in years to come recalled being homesick but he did not recall the cold. When asked to think back on early Kanuga days, he was (then) the retired bishop of Alaska.

Rufus Morgan wrote that the first altar and outdoor chapel were built up above the cottages. They were built of white pine and soon rotted. The next site was down by the stream opposite a flower garden. It was called the Woodland Chapel.

The rail trip from Charleston and pick-up points along the way to Hendersonville was by the "Carolina Special" and those destined for Kanuga let everyone aboard know it. The railroad from all points in the Carolinas gave a special one-way-fare conference rate. It was valid for twenty days.

Laura Smith Ebaugh who had been in charge of girls' physical activities at Camp Capers wrote of her participation in the first five years of Kanuga Conferences. "Daily life at Kanuga was run by a bugler who marked the end of classes, the time for meals, and other activities. The bishop would make announcements in the dining room each day after the blessing was said or sung. The night programs were the delight of all because everyone, young and old, took part. Bishop Finlay was a great raconteur and told ghost stories beautifully, so naturally there was always a ghost story night. There was usually a circus with the bishop acting as master of ceremonies. There were also charades, musical evenings, and square dances.

"Another feature of each early conference was the banquet at the end of the conference period when awards were given, speeches made and songs sung. Mendel Rivers, later a member of

Congress from South Carolina, was toastmaster at the first young people's banquet. He also was elected best all-round boy camper that year." Adult conferences always included a dress-up closing banquet.

Sewanee student Charles Thomas had been a camper at Camp Capers and was in charge of Kanuga's canteen. Moultrie Burns of Camden and Albert Thomas, Jr., of Charleston were assigned to help him as the business that first year quickly grew. Bishop Finlay bought a second-hand Packard topless touring car for their use in bringing canteen and general kitchen food supplies out from Hendersonville. They were the envy of others as they got to miss classes and lectures and cruise over the rough road into the city each day. The canteen was open for a half hour or so after lunch and supper. Thomas said that the canteen in 1928 showed a profit and he was told by Bishop Finlay that the canteen was the only feature of Kanuga that could show a profit and justify it. The money, the bishop told him, would enable those without funds to come to Kanuga.

That first summer the rains came. There were days of unrelenting rain, and as in 1916, Kanuga's dam broke. The dam— Kanuga's third—had been built on a clay bank with mica underneath, which does not form into a water resistant substance. All knew that if the wind should change directions and blow against the dam the pressure of the waves would be such that the dam could not hold. The wind changed during the night. Early in the morning the dam broke. Bishop Finlay's immediate concern was a possible epidemic of some kind if the frogs, fish, and tadpoles were not immediately removed from the drained lakebed. Volunteers worked all day in the mud to clean up the mess. Truckloads of the critters were buried. Bishop Finlay in his early burst of enthusiasm to get the job done had promised to pay 25 cents for each 100 of the dead retrieved. Kanuga would have gone broke then and there if anyone had asked for payment.

Repairing the dam was another story. The dam which washed out was the dam which had replaced the one destroyed by the heavy rains of 1916. The old and much-traveled Brevard highway which ran just below the dam likewise was washed out and would be costly for the county to repair. Consequently, in March 1929, while repair was in progress, the county officials threatened an injunction to insure the repair was at least in part concrete and directed the county engineer to inspect the construction. The problem was resolved but with statewide adverse publicity for the new Episcopal conference center. The cost of the new dam was a whopping $4,113.

The registration blank for this first Kanuga-based summer camp and conference season was the schedule that would be the basic Kanuga format for some years to come.

Registration Blank for 1928
Young People's Camp (Camp Ellison Capers) .....June 16–29
Teacher Training &
*   Woman's Auxiliary Conference ....July 2–13*
Junior Boys' Camp...July 2–13
Junior Girls' Camp ....July 16–25
Clergy Conference ....July 16–25

Fees as follows:
Young People's Camp $20.00
Teacher Training Conference & Woman's Auxiliary ..$20.00
Junior Boys' Camp $15.00
Junior Girls' Camp $15.00
Clergy Conference $12.00
*   Guest Period from the closing of Clergy Conference*
*   to early September ($1.50 per day)*

Bishop Finlay at the end of the 1929 summer season told the managers, "It has been operated for two seasons without any organized management." Rufus Morgan was officially designated Secretary-Treasurer and Business Manager at the October Board of Managers' meeting that fall. Rufus Morgan became a legend for his ability to make every dollar count. Missioner rector of St. John's, Columbia, and a full-time diocesan worker from 1931 to 1940, he would devote considerably more time to Kanuga in the future and his diocese was reimbursed $1,000 a year by Kanuga for this exchange of duties. He was the natural choice because Morgan and Finlay had been together from the beginning of the North Carolina venture and had confidence in each other.

In 1931, about a quarter-mile from the hotel, they built a boys' camp which could house boys during Kanuga-sponsored summer camps and which during August could be operated on a commercial basis. They built two log buildings at a cost of $675.

These buildings were for assembly and for dining (Kirk Arms) when used for other than Kanuga camping. And they built several "shacks" which would accommodate 18 campers each. The commercial camp initially was operated by Columbia attorney James Perry. Perry had been a Boy Scout executive when he was in law school and earlier had done some personal legal work for Finlay. He stayed twelve years with the camp. "We made money on the camp. We charged $60 a boy and I had my son there and I paid $60 for him and Bishop Finlay talked Ann, my wife, into running the entertainment at Kanuga Inn at that time," he later wrote. The $60 camp price was much below that of other camps in the area at this time.

The 1931 season was a financial success. Attendance at conferences totaled about 743: Young People's Service League, 225; junior camps, 312; and adult and clergy conferences, 206. During guest period they were full to capacity. A new diving tower was built and some time in the summer of 1931 a floating platform with a hand-cranking propulsion device found itself on the lake taking people for rides. It was named "Noah's Ark." The bugle tradition was this year extended to a daily news sheet, *The Kanuga Bugle*. Edited and prepared by Sadie Watters, it contained news stories, cartoons, jokes, and announcements, and was distributed on the dining-room porch after dinner.

In a collection of Kanuga reminiscences dated 1979, Miss Lucy Fletcher wrote: "Marie Watters (Colton) who was 9, 10, or 14 said she and her brother Jack had to 'turn the crank' of the mimeograph machine, frequently in their wet bathing suits after afternoon swims, to have them ready by the time supper was over." Miss Fletcher also told the interesting story of a candlelight service tradition where they "proceeded to the lakeside led by vested choir singing *Light of Light* and all lifted lighted candles forming a cross of fire. This continued until sometime in the late 1940s when natives of the area said it was barbaric and reminded them of the Ku Klux Klan."[3]

Also, in 1931, a fine team of horses with wagon and harness was purchased. They also purchased twelve pigs at the opening of the season which they butchered and used. Their vegetable garden provided some help in keeping kitchen costs down. The old truck was traded in for a new one. Work progressed on walks and the old foot bridge across the arm of the lake was replaced. The financial condition at the end of the year would have been even better had the Citizens Bank of Hendersonville not closed with some 700 Kanuga dollars in it.

Both 1932 and 1933 saw a considerable falling off in numbers of those attending conferences and guest periods. During these depression years it was necessary to borrow each year in order to carry on repairs and property improvements, pay the salary of the caretaker and wages for workers, and pay insurance. Each year the loans were paid back at the close of the season, except in 1932 and 1933 when the income was low. In those lean years Kanuga Conferences Association carried forward for two years an indebtedness of $3,675.

During the 1932 lean year, the Board of Managers and the trustees added 400 acres at a price of $6,800 to the Kanuga holdings. One of the early great needs of Kanuga was an adequate and safe water supply. It was recognized from the very beginning of the endeavor that Kanuga would be required to acquire more land to protect the existing water supply and to expand the watershed. They borrowed with three yearly payments ahead.

At the time of this financial low ebb the Kanuga managers and trustees in 1934 had another major financial decision to make. Should they again borrow to buy some unexpectedly available land? The land became available for purchase with the death of C. Gresham and his widow's desire for an estate settlement.

Her husband had loaned George Stephens the money Stephens used for his part of the final $8,500 Kanuga loan package when Kanuga Conferences took possession of the property. It was a personal note jointly held with Kanuga Conferences Association with an unspecified payment due date. The executor of the estate was informed that the reason such a favorable note was issued to Stephens was because he had befriended Gresham in a business arrangement many years earlier. In the arrangement, Gresham had benefitted some $35,000 to possibly $40,000. When Mrs. Gresham was given this information she was agreeable to a friendly settlement that would reduce the face value of the note she was holding.

The complicated plan that would permit the land purchase was for Stephens to purchase the old Kanuga Lake, Inc. bonds at the going rate of ten cents on the dollar, wipe out his personal underwritings, and repay the Gresham estate at an agreed-to settlement of $3,200. (Stephens had already made some cash payments on this loan.) This would permit Kanuga to buy approximately 390 acres for $5,000. Kanuga attorney G. H. Valentine concurred that the complicated plan was feasible. The sale was concluded and the Kanuga property was increased to 1,190 acres. This purchase included the summit of what is called Wolf Mountain. While land acquisition at this time was a difficult decision to make and to explain, it proved to be farsighted.

From time to time during the 1930s, land was purchased as the opportunity arose. The acquisitions were from a few hundred acres to small tracts of land to protect springs in some purchases. More that 800 acres were added during the decade of the 1930s bringing the total land site up to 1,200 acres. In the 1930s, mountain land in general was selling for just over $20 an acre.

During this period of the early 1930s several Episcopal families purchased lots adjacent to the Kanuga property. Rufus Morgan bought such a small tract and subdivided it into lots which were purchased by May Hairston, Minna Robertson, and Mrs. Finlay. At this time there was the model of the other conference centers which encouraged private cottage sales and adjacent property development on the part of church members. The managers of Kanuga never seriously pursued this private cottage ownership after the acquisition of the property, although Bishop Finlay had discussed it at his diocesan convention when he was first describing the purposes a conference center would serve in the life of the church.

For the first seven years the only expense to any diocese was a $150 assessment to each and a gift of $100 from the Diocese of North Carolina the first season. Kanuga was self-supporting the first year. Often in the mid-thirties guests would simply wire ahead and say they were arriving at Kanuga on a certain date. Ofttimes when the facilities were fully booked there was no way to head them off and when they arrived they still expected to have accommodations. There were capital outlays from the beginning. These included: a new barn roof, a new garage roof, a new pavilion roof, roofing for some cottages, and a partial roofing of the hotel, and to this list could be added road construction and plumbing renovation. It was obvious that the unattended maintenance problems of over twenty years were now taking their toll. Also, there was the salary of the year-round caretaker.

Summer 1935 was to be the great year. Reservations were high. The Guest Period was when Kanuga made enough money to cover expenses, and to make necessary repairs and improvements. Summer 1935 seemed to be that season until infantile paralysis suddenly appeared. Kanuga did not cancel any of its conferences but did exert caution. Once a person entered the grounds, that person was not permitted to leave the conference center. Not even trips into town were permitted. Parents were informed at the entrance that they would not be permitted to return and visit and some parents when informed of this restriction turned around and took their youngsters home. Also in 1935 the theft of a large number of blankets during the winter forced an unforeseen expenditure of $500.

There were seemingly always major unexpected events during this time in Kanuga's early development. Rufus Morgan writing in 1958 recalled one such event:

> I was up here [at Kanuga] on St. Patrick's Day in 1936 from Columbia where I was living and working then, because for those first 16 years I looked after the business end here and had to come up occasionally. I had been up on the mountain and came back down. There had been rain and then there had been snow and the wind arose and the white pine trees began to fall around the buildings. And I stood and watched them fall, one after another, dodging sometimes, watching them fall and watching the wonder of God's, sometimes we say destructive, but creative hand. Before the storm was over, some 250 trees had fallen around the buildings hardly damaging the buildings at all. [The logs were sawed up in a portable sawmill and stored.]

Summer 1937, was, in fact, the great year. Kanuga's summer program was well established and the format developed during the early 1930s was working well. The conferences in 1937 operated at capacity, the largest being the adult-college conference. During the time that the Rev. John Long Jackson of Charlotte directed it in the late 1930s, about 600 men and women participated. In early 1937, a woman was engaged for general publicity. The annual budget now was just at $50,000. Land purchase indebtedness was being progressively retired and there was a chapel fund of cash and lumber equivalency of about $3,500 that had come about with practically no effort.

The growing optimism for Kanuga was expressed anew in August 1937, following a resolution at the convention of the Diocese of Western North Carolina when action for possible establishment of a junior college at Kanuga was begun. *The Asheville Citizen* gave the story big play with the heading "Plan Junior College at Episcopal Center—Need of Institution at Kanuga Is Stressed by Leaders."

A preliminary committee headed by the Western Carolina diocesan, Robert Emmet Gribbin, concluded that an endowment of at least $300,000 would be required, that the institution would be co-educational, and that the required new buildings would be erected with the idea of using them for summer conference purposes as well. Those involved in the effort initially believed that there were Episcopalians of means willing to give substantial sums to such an endeavor.

The junior college idea had precedence in the Presbyterian Montreat Normal School, which eventually became Montreat-Anderson College. Chartered in 1917, the two-year girls' normal school was in 1933 reorganized as Montreat Junior College and in 1934 became Montreat College with an enrollment of about 200 students. But the Presbyterian institution had, in the person of its first president, Dr. Robert Campbell Anderson, a committee of one for finance—a job he held throughout his tenure.

At Kanuga no Episcopalian stepped forth to organize a finance committee probably because those with knowledge about higher education realized there was no need for such an institution in Hendersonville in 1937. The final word about this proposed institution made unfortunate headline news throughout North and South Carolina a few years later.

In 1938, the Diocese of North Carolina became a participating diocese in the Kanuga Conferences Association. Bishop Finlay called admission "one of the happiest and most significant occasions in the life of our united undertaking.... This will mean that the five Carolina dioceses own and operate the Kanuga Conference ground on the same basis." He added in an editorial to his own diocesan *Piedmont Churchman* announcing this good news that: "So far as we know, Kanuga now represents the largest conference center operated by the Episcopal Church in the United States."

Every summer Bishop Finlay would move his office from Columbia to Kanuga and administer his diocese from there while at the same time directing Kanuga's summer program. His office was a small, odd-shaped room in the Inn, room number 21.

Kirkman George Finlay
1877–1938

What manner of man was this Kirkman George Finlay who even in his own time had become a legend? Bishops John E. Hines of Texas and later Presiding Bishop of the church and Thomas Henry Wright of East Carolina are but a few of the many whose determination to enter the ministry was sealed at a Kanuga camp or conference that assuredly bore his stamp.

Finlay was born October 1, 1877, near Greenville, South Carolina, where his parents had moved from Canada for the mother's health. Diphtheria almost immediately claimed the lives of their five children. Kirkman George's arrival in 1877 somewhat assuaged the family grief as did two other children in the years following. Kirkman George was schooled at Professor Von Fingerlin's private school in Greenville and then took a degree at Furman in 1899. From Furman he went to Sewanee's theological school and there both graduated and chose a girl who would become his wife.[4]

In 1901 he met Miss Lucy Reed of St. George, South Carolina, who was at Sewanee visiting her aunt. After a seminary courtship and getting settled into his first parish, Holy Trinity, at Clemson College—as the city now named Clemson was then called—they were married in 1903. Her parents were James Otey Reed and Elinor Murray Reed. She was a maternal descendant of James George, the founder of St. George, South Carolina. Finlay continued his Clemson ministry until 1907 when he was called to be rector of Trinity Church, Columbia. His appointment at age thirty to this important parish indicates the growing stature of Finlay in the diocese.

The abilities which made Kirkman Finlay such a success in the history of Kanuga are the abilities which also made him a successful rector. At historic Trinity in Columbia, under his guidance the system of rented pews was abolished and the every-member canvass instituted as the basis of financial support.

When World War I came he was given a year's leave of absence from his parish to go to France with the Y.M.C.A. of the American Expeditionary Forces. His Trinity parish ministered to the troops at nearby Camp Jackson and the women's work in the parish was organized to assist in the maintenance of the tuberculosis sanitarium at Ridgeway Camp, at that time a private charitable institution.

When the decision was made in 1920 to divide the Diocese of South Carolina into two dioceses, Finlay was, in 1921, elected bishop-coadjutor of the Diocese of South Carolina, and in October 1922, became the bishop of the new Upper South Carolina jurisdiction. The immediately succeeding years saw a marked expansion of the Women's Auxiliary and the development of the Young People's Service League. He had early learned the importance of having communication networks established to achieve his goals, with individuals personally accepting responsibilities for tasks to be achieved. He had been eminently successful at Trinity parish in this leadership style.

His first episcopal address set his agenda: spread the work of the church in industrial areas, develop the work of the church in rural areas, and expand the work of the church among the Negro population.

When the funding for the Voorhees Normal and Industrial School at Denmark, South Carolina, was discontinued because of the deaths in 1922 of the school's benefactors—Mr. and Mrs. Voorhees—Bishop Finlay helped work out an arrangement for the institution to continue to serve its 500 day and 250 boarding students. Voorhees would become an affiliate of the American Church Institute for Negroes and the two South Carolina dioceses. Its future was secured by this combined diocesan and national Episcopal church affiliation. It would become an expense to his diocese, but the bishop reasoned it was stewardship.

There were, however, some setbacks in his diocesan work. Confirmations declined in the early years of his episcopate. The Rev. A. Rufus Morgan then was selected for an office of general missioner and executive secretary of the diocese largely to take care of parishes whose memberships had declined and were without ministers. Also he was defeated in his efforts to include Negro lay and clergy participation in voting for deputies to General Convention and for bishops. Only in the two South Carolina dioceses were Negroes by 1933 denied this inclusion in diocesan life.

The Finlays had five children: James Alexander who died at age one, Kirkman, Edward Reed, Elinor (Mrs. Leighton Collins), and Marian. His biographer, Mary Hardy Phifer, *Kirkman George Finlay,* 1949, writes that one of the personal joys Kanuga brought to Bishop Finlay was the "Bishop's Cottage" as the house near the end of the lake (Cottage One) was called. There Mrs. Finlay and her mother, Mrs. Reed, to whom the bishop was truly devoted, spent the summers with him. Mrs. Finlay acted as unofficial hostess at the administration building, performing necessary tasks that the fledgling budget could not afford to pay a staff person to do.

Illustrative of the tight budget in these early days is the story of the youngster who, in trying to identify Bishop Finlay among some sixteen other bishops present at one summer conference, said, "I mean the bishop that works at the stables." She relates another story of this same kind. With everyone else busy at something, he drove into Hendersonville to bring a guest out to Kanuga. Thinking the tall kindly man clad in knickerbockers, colored shirt, and battered hat to be a porter or man of all work, the guest gave him a generous tip. This man, who had introduced himself without the titles of office, courteously accepted and deposited the tip in the Chapel Fund box.

Bishop Finlay died at Kanuga of a heart attack, August 27, 1938. He was 61 years old. He had been warned by his doctor the previous summer that he should not push himself too hard. Emmet Gribbin, Jr., and Al Chambliss were on duty when the bishop's secretary came down and told them the bishop had been stricken somehow. They went immediately upstairs to his office and took him to his cottage. He died within a few hours.

Funeral services were held at Trinity Church, Columbia, and he was buried in the churchyard beside the church that had become a part of his life. Kanuga thinks often that he had one life— the life shared with Kanuga. He was bishop of a diocese and was buried accordingly. He had put together a diocese. On January 1, 1923, the meager cash balance of the two South Carolina dioceses were divided and the Diocese of Upper South Carolina was on its own. The diocese weathered the difficult depression years under his leadership as its first bishop and Bishop Finlay was known and respected throughout the church. One accomplishment that could be identified as an epitaph of his work is the fact that in 1935 the entire 367 membership of the First Congregational Church of Columbia, became communicants of the Episcopal church.

At the last meeting of the Kanuga Board of Managers presided over by Bishop Finlay (just a month before his death), a site for the long-proposed chapel had been selected. After his death it was announced that the chapel would be built as a memorial to him. The Upper South Carolina diocesan Finlay memorial address was delivered by Bishop Thomas C. Darst. He commemorated his friend's testament of faith:

> *His religion then was of a very human and practical kind. It was overshadowed by the conviction that God is love, and its practice was controlled by another conviction second only to this: we should love one another as He hath loved us.*

Chapter Four
Chapels

It is not built of costly stone,
With carvings rich and rare,
'Tis made of pine—Kanuga's own—
And knotted everywhere.[1]

Helen Griffith

If the church is going to have a conference center it is going to have a chapel. It accordingly goes without saying that if that conference center is an Episcopal church conference center, that chapel must come early and it must be beautiful. Rufus Morgan writes, "In the first place, from about 1923 on, somehow or other it became my privilege to build the temporary altars for the outdoor services wherever our camps were—whether it was See Off or Camp Transylvania or here at Kanuga."

A chapel fund was begun as early as 1930. In 1936, at the February 20 board meeting, Bishop Finlay raised the question of increasing the rates at Kanuga and building the proposed chapel. There was no direct action taken. However, January 28, 1937, board minutes do indicate the chapel fund had grown to $3,502.72.

At its meeting July 1938, a resolution was adopted stating that the chapel could begin when 90 percent of the funding was in hand. In August, Bishop Finlay presided at the consecration of Calvary Church, Fletcher. The 1859 church had been almost destroyed by a 1935 fire which left only the bell tower, west wall, and entrance standing. The architect in reconstruction had sensitively preserved these old walls and had used the salvageable bricks in the new building to suggest the continuity of the two structures. Bishop Finlay was impressed with the architect's work and stated that he wanted the same architect to design the new chapel which was being considered for Kanuga. The bishop also said at the time that the Kanuga chapel must have both integrity and authenticity. The bishop died seven days following these public remarks but his request in selecting an architect was followed.

The chapel was named the Chapel of the Transfiguration because the idea expressed in the collect for the Transfiguration feast day epitomized what Kanuga had come to mean to a rapidly growing number of Episcopalians who had attended conferences at Kanuga. The substance of that collect is withdrawal and spiritual reflection, and then back to the world for work. Bishop Finlay often spoke and wrote about the mountains as a source of strength. The last editorial he wrote for his diocesan *Piedmont Churchman* shares with the reader the strength that had come to him personally from time in the mountains:

> *A mountain top, a great man, and a vision—this is a significant combination. The mountain top was Sinai; the man, Moses; the Vision, a Tabernacle. It was to be the center of life for his people as they traveled toward the promised land.*[2]

Bishop Finlay's words in retrospect are a description also of how his friends viewed him and his work at Kanuga.

Kanuga board minutes, in September 1938, report that a committee was directed to ask S. Grant Alexander, architect of Calvary Church, Fletcher, to draw the plans if he would accept two stipulations. The first was a $10,000 budget limitation. The other was that he use timber that would be cut from Kanuga's forest and the timber that had been stored and saved from the great 1936 St. Patrick's Day storm. The following month the minutes record the architect's acceptance of the offer and that the board was assured his plans would be under $10,000. By January 1939, some $9,000 was on hand for chapel construction with the understanding of the board that this would include both the architect's fee and all promotional fund-raising expenses.

The Asheville architect selected, S. Grant Alexander, was a native of Inverness Shire, Scotland, and had received his education and professional training in his native country. *The Asheville Citizen,* at the time of his death in January 1953, stated, "Prior to making his home in America he practiced his profession in Scotland where he designed and supervised restoration and

expansion of that country's historical homes and buildings."
Alexander was a Fellow of the Royal Institute of British Architects
and a Fellow of the Faculty of Surveyors of Scotland, and was
awarded the Order of the British Empire for his work during the
war. Family tradition claims that the Alexanders are collateral
descendants of the Scottish king, Robert the Bruce.[3]

Alexander came with his parents and one sister to the United
States in the early 1920s, his sister stating that their parents were
seeking more opportunity for their children and a more desirable
climate. In Asheville, Alexander formed the architectural firm of
S. Grant Alexander & Associates, a company that at one time
included both his father and his son, Ludovic J. Grant Alexander.

Carolina Architecture & Allied Arts, 1940—a privately printed
collection of Asheville and surrounding area buildings the com-
pilers thought to be significant—included three buildings that
Alexander designed: the three-story Monte Vista Manor in Black
Mountain, the office for the Beverly Hills Company, Asheville, and
the Asheville residence alteration for Mr. and Mrs. W. H. Lashley.[4]
He also designed other buildings in that area, including Grace
Baptist Church in West Asheville. Alexander was employed as
architect and designed the parish house for Grace Episcopal
Church in Asheville, but he died before the work on that building
was begun.[5] He designed both a Baptist and a Presbyterian
church in Marshall, North Carolina.

It was necessary to cut many corners in construction costs
for the new chapel resulting in structural weakness that caused
the walls to lean out as the high roof was put in place. The new
board president, Bishop Robert E. Gribbin of the Diocese of
Western North Carolina, who had been elected to that job after the
death of Bishop Finlay, told the building committee, in July 1939,
that he had stopped timber cutting and had, in effect, brought the
construction job to a temporary halt. Piers were not as strong as
they should be, the bishop told the committee, and the walls were
bulging. The bishop had sought advice from the South Carolina
architect who had built the Episcopal church in Aiken (a Mr. Olan)
and he had suggested ways to solve the construction problem.
Metal support rods stretching from one outside nave wall to the
other were inserted to bear the stress the wooden buttresses were
not able to sustain. The rods are still in place. It is possible that
this was Alexander's first large-scale American-building experi-

ence with wood, and that he was not aware that the tensile strength of white pine was unlike the hardwood timber he had used as a young architect in Great Britain. Alexander also provided the board written plans to solve the bulging problem and injected a plea that this construction delay not be long because it imposed an unemployment hardship on the construction workers.

At this July 1939 meeting, the board decided to secure additional expert advice both on determining exactly what the structural defects were and how to fix responsibility, indicating the depth of feeling about the chapel construction problem.

At this same board meeting, a proposed memorial window to the Rt. Rev. Junius M. Horner, Bishop of Western North Carolina from 1896 to 1933, from church women was accepted. The reason presented to the board for the stained glass window which was going to be out of character with a building not designed for colored windows was that such a light-diffusing device was necessary and that they simply wanted to honor the bishop with such a window. It was so ordered. Interestingly, the artist who designed the window placed stigmata in the hands of Christ as he portrayed the Transfiguration story in the window. The window had to be altered to remove the stigmata which is not appropriate in a Transfiguration story. The wounds were a result of the crucifixion while the Transfiguration story was at the beginning of Christ's ministry. The memorial window was dedicated June 14, 1940, at a service held in conjunction with the 18th annual meeting of the Woman's Auxiliary of the Diocese of Western North Carolina.

In quick order other memorials followed the Bishop Horner memorial window. The pulpit was given in 1939 in honor of Mr. Pendleton by the Woman's Auxiliary of the Church of the Advent in Spartanburg, where he was rector. The small credence shelf to the right of the altar is a memorial to Margaret Ashe. A young man who was in love with Margaret Ashe when she died as a senior at the University of South Carolina in 1939 collected contributions from several of her friends to have the credence shelf given in her honor. Pews were made by and under the supervision of Rufus Huneycutt on the grounds by Kanuga workers and staff. The pews have brass plaques on the ends identifying the recipients in whose honor the pews were given. A wall plaque identifies Christ

Church, Millwood, Virginia, as donor of the four original light fittings. The light fittings were handmade and the only record to indicate their origin identifies "a Mr. Reid" as either the maker or supplier. Laura Ebaugh, in a letter June 28, 1979, states that part of the church furnishings came from an early Etowah chapel. The story seems creditable and this no doubt was Gethsemane Church which was built at nearby Bowman's Bluff and then was disbanded in 1907. Some of the furnishings were then taken to little St. John-the-Baptist, the church in Upward (near Hendersonville), and then when that church was disbanded those furnishings are known to have been scattered.

The building committee met in the chapel when it held its meeting in July 1939. A service in the uncompleted chapel is recorded for July 1939, when some two-hundred-fifty persons attending an adult, college, and clergy conference held a communion service there. The chapel cornerstone was put in place June 30, 1940, at 5:00 p.m.

At the board meeting in January 1940 in attempting to assess the total chapel construction costs, the board concluded that $716.91 would be the assigned value of all Kanuga-cut timber used in the chapel construction. The actual cost of the chapel then was $12,110.20, including moving two cottages (numbers seven and eight) and insurance. The cost assigned to the chapel construction alone was $11,000 and was so stated in the minutes, only a ten percent overrun.

The Chapel of the Transfiguration was dedicated July 19, 1942. Everybody attended. Bishop Gribbin of Western North Carolina was in charge of the service. The clergy taking part included Bishop Jackson of Louisiana, Bishop Thomas of South Carolina, Bishop Darst of East Carolina, and the Rev. Dr. Pendleton, the Rev. Rufus Morgan, the Rev. Louis C. Melcher, and the Rev. John Pinckney. William Robertson directed the 60-voice choir and played the borrowed organ. No mention of the architect was given in *The Asheville Times'* account of the dedication service; recognition was not accorded the architect in the printed dedication program.

The organ borrowed for the chapel dedication service was from Clemson although details are not recorded. At the meeting of the board the day following the dedication, a resolution was adopted stating that chapel offerings exceeding chapel operating expenses should be put in an organ fund as a thank offering for the services of Mr. and Mrs. William G. Robertson of the Diocese of East Carolina.

Scotty and Mummy Robertson were listed among the faithful in their music contributions to the conferences. A committee was appointed at the February 1944 board meeting to check on the possibility of getting a government-surplus organ. Nothing came of this effort. Eighteen hundred dollars had been budgeted for an organ in 1947, and an electronic Hammond organ was purchased although it was $425 above budget. A tablet honoring the Robertsons was installed on the instrument.

In 1957, steel channel supports under the eaves and through the transepts of the chapel were installed to prevent further movement of the walls. New roofing was put on this same year. There had been for a few years some leaking necessitating a certain amount of patching in each of those preceding years. The exterior of the chapel was stained and the trim painted at the same time. This was the first repair to the chapel since its construction. The hinged kneelers were installed in 1963. Prior to that time there were cushion kneelers.

A 1915 Estey reed organ was given to Kanuga and placed in the chapel in 1992. The handcrafted oak-console, two-manual instrument with 15 stops, was built for a Vermont church and later purchased by Marylyn and Luther Wade of Charlotte. They had it rebuilt and used it in their home where Marylyn, a professional organist, used it for practice. Their gift was dedicated as a memorial to the Wades' parents the weekend their St. Martin's parish was at Kanuga for its Parish Family Weekend, September 11–13, 1992. After fifty years the Chapel of the Transfiguration had a real organ.

The development of Kanuga's other early chapel—named in 1941 Chapel of St. Francis of Assisi—has been gradual. From the time a chapel was located opposite the flower garden down by the stream this woodland chapel and setting became important to many. Rufus Morgan wrote: "Some of our friends heard us say we wished we could have a permanent altar of stone and they quietly contributed enough to build it. When my sister, Miss Lucy Morgan, head of Penland School of Handicrafts, heard that we had built the stone altar, she offered the services of her teacher of ceramics, Miss Becky Jamerson, to make a frontal of clay. We planned together the composition, using the figures of St. Francis and two of his early disciples." With the help of Bascom Hoyle of Penland, the fired-clay St. Francis frontal was installed June 23, 1942. The iron cross and candlesticks were made at the John C. Campbell Folk School, Brasstown, North Carolina. New benches were installed in 1963. The benches were mounted on Boliden salt-treated poles, shaped as rustic pew ends. The seats were made of redwood. They were scheduled to last twenty-five years.

The outdoor chapel was, in August 31, 1933, to be the scene of the first ordination at Kanuga. It was scheduled to be outdoors because at the time that was Kanuga's only chapel. The ordinand was a Kanuga camper of many seasons and Kanuga was a convenient place for him, his Seneca, South Carolina, family, and Bishop Finlay to get together. A torrential rain forced the ceremony to be moved into the rotunda of the hotel. The bishop of Cuba, the Rt. Rev. H. R. Hulse, participated with Bishop Finlay in the rite which ordained John Elbridge Hines deacon. In 1965, he was elected Presiding Bishop of the Protestant Episcopal Church in the United States.

The canons of the Episcopal church place all Episcopal services in any church or chapel in the geographical area encompassed by that diocese under the jurisdiction of the resident bishop. Bishop of Western North Carolina, George Henry, had strong feelings about churchmanship and stated the norm in a statement he drafted and placed on the wall in the chapel: "It has been the aim and purpose of Kanuga to continue his (Bishop Finlay's) simplicity of living and worship. Therefore, any questions as to placement of furnishings, conduct of services and music, must be referred to the priest-in-charge, appointed by the Bishop of Western North Carolina." The statement also reminded the reader, "It has been the custom since Kanuga Conferences began to hold twilight services on the lakeside, weather permitting, except during Guest Period."

From its initial construction until midway in the 1970s, the chapel served Kanuga well. However, the variations in liturgical practice in the 1970s were such that conference leaders with increasing frequency chose other places with more flexible seating and altar arrangements for worship services. The New York Rambusch church-design studio was selected in 1977 to investigate ways the chapel could be made more adaptable to the changing modes of worship. Willy Malarcher who also had taught at the Christian Education Conferences for the past two years was, by coincidence, the Rambusch design consultant. His first comments were, "From my experience with two summer conferences, and also sitting in on the sessions of the summer planning committee, the chapel seems to be mainly avoided because of its inflexibility."

Robert L. Haden, Jr., board member, program committee chairman, and rector of St. John's Church, Charlotte, was asked to chair a committee to work through this problem which at the time carried the strong emotions attached to the concurrent prayer-book revision.[6] Rambusch prepared optional designs for their consideration.

In the summer of 1977, the conference center experimented with the Rambusch chapel proposals. Kanuga guests responded differently to seating and altar changes made in the chapel on the test basis. A questionnaire showed that 86 percent of the summer conference respondents felt the changes made the liturgical service more meaningful. It allowed worshippers to gather around a centrally-placed altar that was visible to all. But Guest Period respondents were 90 percent opposed to the changes. However, one result of the summer experiment was increased use of the chapel in contrast with the previous two years when it virtually was not used by conference participants.

"I do not think a BVM (Blessed Virgin Mary) statue will make it at Kanuga. St. Francis might make it," wrote chapel committee chairman, Bob Haden, to his committee when he presented its suggestions for their consideration. He rephrased it a bit in his committee report to the Board of Directors in 1977 when he said that "these measures were thought to be the solution to pleasing 'both sides' of chapel users—those who favor the traditional chapel as it is and those who favor making some changes which allow flexibility in additional conference use." The board concurred.

In 1986, further chapel changes transformed this summer chapel into a year-round place of assembly and worship. The overhead of the Transfiguration Chapel was insulated. And the chapel was heated. The heat was turned on first for the See The Leaves Guest Period. During Thanksgiving Guest Period, 249 people attended a Eucharist in a heated chapel. At this same time, new electrical circuitry was put in place to accommodate increased lighting and permit installation of ceiling fans.

Counselors-in-training at Camp Kanuga, in the summer of 1983, rebuilt a lakeside chapel for this camp. It was dedicated as St. Andrew's Chapel on July 17 by the Rt. Rev. William A. Beckham, bishop of Upper South Carolina and Kanuga board chairman. The chapel is used for vespers, Sunday services, and special events. St. Andrew's Chapel was originally constructed in the summer of 1962 and consecrated the following year. The counselors-in-training in 1983 enlarged the site, added 23 wooden benches built from logs, and made a fireplace. The group worked for three weeks, at least two hours a day, on the project. They also cleared trails to the site and built a new bridge to cross a creek that flows beside the chapel.

The Lakeside Chapel at the conference center is near the place where people began gathering for worship on the hillside facing the lake in 1928. The chapel today is closer to the Inn than previous lakeside chapels and the site permits additional seating at the upper concrete deck and also allows wheelchair access. Approximately 200 people can sit on the benches which are made from South American mahogany. The speaker's podium stands on a stage built of cedar that is large enough to accommodate large group activities. In 1983 the cross on the far lakeshore was moved 75 yards southwest to its present location so it is now in direct view from the lakefront chapel. The present chapel was a gift from Kanuga board member and property chairman Jack Jones and his wife Phyllis and Mrs. Eleanor T. McCullough and Charles E. Thomas, all of Christ Church, Greenville, South Carolina. The chapel was dedicated August 1, 1987, with the Rev. Charles G. vonRosenberg officiating.

The Rev. Robert Haden has observed that each chapel possesses its own special atmosphere, enabling a variety of spiritual experiences. He told this writer:

> The people of St. John's Parish, Charlotte, have been coming to Kanuga for parish weekends for twenty years. On most weekends we utilize all of the chapels.... We leave the 'Holy Mountain' spiritually refreshed, having worshipped God all over the place.

ӘꞪᎦ

13. Bishop Kirkman Finlay in rotunda of Kanuga Inn showing the 1935 Cantey Johnson memorial cross. The altar was moved later to the Chapel of the Transfiguration.

(Photograph: Bayard Wootten, Chapel Hill)

14. (Top) Bishop Finlay's family at Kanuga for unveiling of portrait executed by Mrs. Hugh Walker of Greenville, South Carolina. Left to right are Marian Finlay, Kirkman Finlay, Jr., Mrs. K. G. Finlay, Edward Reed Finlay, Jr., Caroline Knowlton Finlay, and Mr. and Mrs. Edward Reed Finlay. Not present are daughter Elinor and son Kirkman. (1953 photo)

15. (Right) Elinor Murray Reed, "Grandma Reed." "She always won the fancy dress ball." (Mrs. Reed was Bishop Finlay's mother-in-law) (circa 1930s)

16. (Top) The Rev. A. Rufus Morgan, 1886–1983 (Kanuga Conferences director, 1939–1943) "The Modern Moses" drawing by niece, Marjorie Weatherly Ostborg

17. (Left) The Rt. Rev. John A. Pinckney, 1905–1972 (Kanuga Conferences director, 1943–1950)
(Photograph: Charles Old Studio, Columbia)

18. Camp Capers, Transylvania, 1925.

19. Camp Capers, 1925 Faculty stunt, "Kingdom of Insania," with Bishop Finlay as King (seated, center). An early advocate of human dignity, Finlay eliminated the practice of Black Face portrayals early in Kanuga history. (See page 67)

THE WEATHER
NORTH CAROLINA: Rain Sunday and Sunday night; Monday fair.

THE SUNDAY CITIZEN

"DEDICATED TO THE UPBUILDING OF WESTERN NORTH CAROLINA"

ESTABLISHED 1868 ASHEVILLE, N. C., SUNDAY MORNING, APRIL 22, 1928 52 PAGES

Paid Circulation, March, 1928
Daily Average....18,788
Sunday Average....19,503

EPISCOPAL CHURCH CENTER PLANNED AT KANUGA

✛ ✛   ✛ ✛   ✛ ✛   ✛ ✛   ✛ ✛   ✛ ✛   ✛ ✛

20. Headline in the Asheville paper, *The Sunday Citizen*, on April 22, 1928, announcing the plans to purchase 400 acres as a conference and camp center for the Episcopal church in the Carolinas. Opening sentence reads, "Kanuga Lake, near Hendersonville, long noted for its setting of rugged mountain beauty, is expected to become one of the great religious conference centers of the country."

CONFERENCES WILL BE HELD IN JUNE FOR 4 DIOCESES

Plans To Purchase 400 Acres And Village Are Approved

FUND IS ALREADY HALF SUBSCRIBED

Bishop John G. Murray And Associates Back Program

21. Side entrance to the Inn, circa 1960.

22. Guests enjoying swimming, circa 1950.

23. Pavilion showing 1970 storm damage.

24. (Top) Evelyn and Bill Verduin, 1993. (Willard P. Verduin was Kanuga Conferences executive director, 1950–1963)

25. (Left) Edgar Hartley, Jr., 1919–1982 (Kanuga Conferences executive director, 1966-1982)

Chapter Five
The Forties

*The old pavilion was a great institution. I never felt that
I had arrived at Kanuga until I went into the interior of the
pavilion and took a deep breath. For the pavilion had a
smell of its own due to the accumulated odors seeping
into the floor and walls from the lake underneath, from
the bodies of young prancing athletes, from the old
costumes that were stored for plays and parties. The
pavilion smell was not offensive. It was just different. No
one who ever smelled it will ever forget it. No one who
never smelled it could ever imagine it.*[1]

Berkeley Grimball

In the late 1930s the nation's economy was still in depression, the Great Depression as it came to be called. Each of the
bishops in his own diocese had unmet institutional building and
repair needs—not unlike those at Kanuga—which the depression
years had imposed. While Kanuga had had highest priority—a
cause—with Bishop Finlay, the bishops who followed him, while
much interested in Kanuga, were understandably concerned first
with their own dioceses.

When Bishop Robert E. Gribbin of the Diocese of Western
North Carolina was elected president of the Kanuga Board of
Managers to replace Bishop Finlay, the chief priority of the board
was the erection and completion of the long-planned chapel. The
need was evident and those who had learned to love and support
Kanuga readily joined in the endeavor. The chapel had no heat
and no thought was even given to such an idea. Screens to keep
out summer insects were acceptable.

Kanuga was a summer place and inconveniences associated with old plumbing, unheated bedrooms and bathrooms, leaking roofs, and makeshift kitchen appliances, were all tolerable camping experiences for the few weeks of summer when everything else associated with Kanuga was so great. In fact, for many, part of the camping ethos was roughing it in the mountains. Both the nights and the water—outside and inside the hotel—were cold.

Along with the election of a new board president, an Executive Committee had been established in October 1938 to "handle matters coming up between meetings of the Board of Managers"— that is to say, a committee to do the work previously entrusted to Bishop Finlay. The committee would be the board president, vice-president, and secretary-treasurer, together with the directors of the various conferences and camps as associate members. Rufus Morgan would continue as secretary-treasurer and business manager. Morgan had requested this responsibility as a testimony to his long Kanuga interest and close working relationship with Bishop Finlay. "I felt I knew his mind and what he would have done under the circumstances. I was anxious that this be continued," he later wrote of this transition period.

The Executive Committee's first meeting—with five bishops present plus Mr. Morgan and Mr. Pinckney—had an agenda which dealt with the effect the Charleston, South Carolina, school closing date changes might have on Kanuga's Young People's Conference and setting the dates of other various conferences. The charges to be affixed at the Layman's Conference to the room and board billings of those who would elect to stay at Kanuga an extra day were discussed and a request from Seventh-Day Adventists who wanted to rent the property for a week in 1940 was considered. They also devoted time deciding how the price of Kanuga lumber should be figured in calculating the total cost of the chapel.

Also on that agenda was how dining-room scholarships should be handled. This was a high priority with the bishops and was discussed at length. Seven young people from each participating diocese were selected by their bishops for dining-room scholarships. They attended a conference, and as the scholarship title implied, worked in food services. The only cost to the students was a $2.25 registration fee for the two-week conference they would serve. There was an agreement that two or three always would be boys to ensure enough heavy-duty workers. The scholarships were both prized and sought after.

Rufus Morgan reported that 1939 was the worst financial year Kanuga ever had. It was compounded by the fact that no longer was there a chapel fund that could be used as a revolving fund for the money needed immediately before conference money began to accumulate.

The Rev. Rufus Morgan continued on a year-to-year election as director of Kanuga and as business manager and treasurer. In 1940 a Committee on General Programs was formed and that committee elected the dietician, head of the waterfront, hotel manager, manager of the canteen, head nurse, hostess, and bookkeeper. The committee arranged the entire yearly program and nominated the directors of conferences and retreats and the director of the guest period.

While the early 1940s minutes of the Executive Committee and the minutes of the Board of Managers indicate much attention to details, little attention is given to long-range program planning or to maintenance other than getting through the summer. Examples of Board of Managers' action—twenty members present including three bishops—are the following from Tuesday, July 23, 1940:

— *Mr. Morgan reported on the loan made to Kanuga which was authorized by the board at the last meeting.... All outstanding debts were explained. The approximate total indebtedness of Kanuga at the present time was $20,000.*

— *Bishop Gribbin stated that an offer to give a classroom for the clergy had been made. This classroom to be in appreciation of Dr. Pendleton's services and to be called the Pendleton Hall. The motion was made and adopted that the offer be accepted with great appreciation.*

— *That the following named directors for the season of 1941 be elected:*

> *Junior Conference—the Rev. A. Rufus Morgan*
> *Young People's Conference—The Rev. John A. Pinckney*
> *Adult Conference—The Rt. Rev. John L. Jackson*
> *Clergy Conference—The Rt. Rev. Thomas C. Darst*
> *Midget Camp—Mrs. M. D. Whisnant*
> *Boys' Camp—Mr. James Y. Perry*

— *Mr. Morgan brought up the matter of changing the insurance on the chapel from the company which had it now to the Church Fire Insurance Company at a rate approxi-*

mately 36 percent lower. Motion carried.

— *Mr. Morgan brought up the matter of electric re-wiring for the whole plant. He stated that the cost would be approximately $1,000. The motion was adopted that the matter be referred to the Committee on General Programs.*

— *Mr. Perry suggested that a recreational building was needed at the Boys' Camp. He stated that it could be built from proceeds from the Boys' Camp. The motion was made and adopted that the matter be referred to the Committee on General Programs.*

The Rev. John L. Jackson who had for years been director of the very successful summer Adult Conference was elected bishop of Louisiana in 1940. He was asked to continue on the Kanuga board. He was affectionately known in his Charlotte parish and by Kanuga friends as "The Big Wheel." As a member of the Board of Managers, he began in 1942 to urge a change in administrative procedure for Kanuga. Acting on his suggestion the board engaged the services of Reed S. Salley of Columbia to make an inspection of the grounds and buildings and report on the condition of the wiring and possible fire hazards. At the same time, the bishop persuaded the board to secure a loan to pay off the $27,000 indebtedness and that this loan be designated as a capital account and be amortized over a period of years thus freeing up incoming funds for expenditures needed immediately. At the same time that a capital improvements account was set up, the board established a Finance and Property Committee to supervise finances and to execute plans for the maintenance and improvement of the property.

Also, Bishop Jackson secured the establishment of a Kanuga Association. This was an effort to formalize the interested friends and churches into a membership organization which would make annual contributions to the Association and accordingly provide funding for continuing improvements to the property. Also it was the purpose of this association to better inform and interest Episcopalians throughout the South in Kanuga's program.

Further changes were in order for Kanuga when in July 1943 a "Recommended Plan Governing the Board of Managers" was adopted. While not major in scope, the plan did begin to alter the yearly elections of almost everyone who performed services or held responsibilities at Kanuga. The Finance and Property Committee would serve three years and would report yearly in writing to the board. A Program Committee consisting of the board president, superintendent, and the directors and deans of the conferences and camps would plan and coordinate Kanuga conferences and camps. The board performing committee work was decreasing and the role of the superintendent was being enlarged. (In the early history of Kanuga, the title superintendent and director are at times used interchangeably.)

The board, in July 1943, accepted the resignation of Rufus Morgan as superintendent—a job he had been elected to each year since Bishop Finlay's death. He and Mrs. Morgan were invited to be honored guests during the Guest Period "so long as they both shall live." Morgan had a year earlier asked to be relieved of his responsibilities but the board had persuaded him to stay one more year.

His position was offered to M. D. Whisnant, director of Thompson's Orphanage and Training Institute, an institution of the Diocese of North Carolina, but he declined. "Kanuga has never recovered from a debt which was incurred shortly after the property was purchased," he told the board. In personal correspondence with his bishop, the Rt. Rev. Edwin A. Penick, he said that there was no consensus about Kanuga's place in the family of church institutions and until that foundation was established he could see no professional future for himself and his family at Kanuga. The Rev. Harvey Simmonds was then asked to accept the job of superintendent and he too declined. Greenville rector John A. Pinckney then accepted the position as a summer assignment. Again, a one-year personnel program was the only solution.

Early in 1944, after all the debts from the previous year had been paid, Bishop Jackson called attention to the fact that one-third of the outstanding indebtedness, or about $8,000, was paid off in 1943. Walter J. Grace, a Macon, Georgia, attorney and civic leader, who came to Kanuga during the Guest Period, wrote to the board suggesting names of laymen interested in helping Kanuga liquidate its long-time indebtedness. The board's reaction to this offer was a suggestion that those interested in this might get together during the Guest Period and set up an organization. After more thought, the board asked for a special committee to pursue Grace's offer.

The Rev. B. Duvall Chambers offered to donate a bond towards this purpose and urged that any fund-raising be undertaken during the approaching Fourth War Bond Drive. Mr. Chambers' thoughts on how the Kanuga appeal would be enhanced by this timing are not recorded. Grace set about identifying Kanuga property needs and supplied a comprehensive report on what he thought was needed. There is no record that any formal action was taken concerning this report.

Also early in 1944, Kanuga received a formal request from the Diocese of Louisiana to become one of the participating dioceses of Kanuga Conferences. The request was received at the February 1, 1944, board meeting and was referred to the Executive Committee for review and referred back to the Board of Managers. A change in the constitution would be necessary before any diocese could be admitted. Also there was the broader question of the future character and religious emphasis of this Carolina conference center. An example of one aspect of this concern is that at this same meeting and before they formally received the resolution to act on Louisiana's request, the board passed a resolution prohibiting intoxicating liquors and Sunday public cardplaying so "church people may live together in the spirit of Christian fellowship." The New Orleans Episcopalians were being reminded of Carolina churchmanship.

The Louisiana diocese in 1944 went on record as expressing "its willingness to assume membership as a participating diocese in the management and ownership of Kanuga Conference at Kanuga Lake, near Hendersonville, N.C., if this is acceptable to the Board of Managers of Kanuga." Bishop Jackson's diary in 1945 records being "welcomed into the family of Dioceses directing the work of this Conference Center, and we are asked to elect members of the Board of Managers." Records are inconclusive defining this relationship but from this date the terminology "owning and participating dioceses" is frequently found throughout the 1950s in Kanuga correspondence among the bishops.

The Board of Managers met at Kanuga in July 1945 during the conference period. There was good news to report. Kanuga had two new classrooms for 1945. Classroom #2 was named Finlay Hall and classroom #3 was named Hunter Hall. One was the gift of the Rev. B. Duvall Chambers and the second from the Adult Conference which Bishop Jackson had directed the previous summer. James Wilson Hunter was a popular conference teacher who came to Kanuga from Louisville, Kentucky. He was in 1949 named bishop of Wyoming and served that diocese for twenty years. (Pendleton Hall, 1940, was #1.)

The five-year-old Kanuga Association at this same board meeting received the board's thanks for several new projects that the Kanuga Association had financed: a new water pump and a newly-painted kitchen, both recognized to be long needed. Mr. Pinckney responded to this upbeat summer by again raising the question of a school that would utilize the Kanuga facilities.

A year later, at a mid-summer meeting, 1946, Bishop Gravatt reported to the board that he had discussed the school idea with several educators and concluded by saying simply that the idea was still being discussed. Board minutes did not identify who was involved in the discussion. Bishop John J. Gravatt of the Diocese of Upper South Carolina was now Kanuga president, Bishop Gribbin having asked to be relieved because of health.

At this mid-summer meeting of the Board of Managers, Bishop Gravatt presented Jackson Hall (a memorial to the Rt. Rev. John Long Jackson) to Kanuga, "the gift of many friends of Kanuga, who without concerted effort or solicitation of any kind, had individually contributed funds to make this classroom possible." This became Kanuga's fourth classroom. Like the other classrooms, this was a frame, free-standing, summer-use building. In contrast to this good news was the assortment of mounting maintenance problems: the need to re-roof the cottages with fire-proof shingles at a cost of $187 per cottage roof; the need for noise amelioration in the dining room by the installation of acoustical tile; the problems of last-minute conference cancellations and reconciling the loss of income and the desire also to maintain the good will of the individuals involved; and, of course, the continuing need for staff salary increases.

Attendance at Kanuga Conferences throughout the 1940s was good. "The old Inn was an interesting and comfortable building but it really was a fire trap. and if it had caught fire there really would have been a lot of roasted Episcopalians. Every year during the conferences we had a 'so called' fire drill. The drill consisted of all the campers lining up from the Inn to the lake and passing a water bucket up from the lake to the porch of the Inn. The amount of water provided would not have put out a match," wrote Berkeley Grimball about these days. As he calls himself, this "Irascible Ol' Curmudgeon" and his wife Emily have been

Kanuga devotees for over forty years.[2] (Berkeley Grimball was the key figure in merging Porter Military Academy, Gaud School, and Watt School into Porter-Gaud School with a campus on Charleston's beautiful Albemarle Point.)

In early 1947, Bishop Jackson told the board that his health would not permit him to direct the Adult, College, and Clergy Conferences after the coming summer. This conference had been the Kanuga headline conference because it was the conference for adults who were the parish and diocesan leaders. All recognized that this was true in considerable measure due to Bishop Jackson, the person, the organizer, the teacher, and the speaker. For many adults this summer conference was Kanuga. The conferences provided as many courses as possible of both a technical and inspirational nature. The faculty was carefully selected and many people were sent to the conferences by their parishes for a special course of instruction in some field of church work. From 9:00 a.m. to 1:00 p.m. there were five or six courses to select from each hour. Afternoons were free for recreation and there was a 7:15 twilight service by the lake. And 8:15 p.m. was program time. This was from the earliest days something very special. The program time was the origin of many nostalgic tales of Kanuga. Those smelly old costumes did indeed come out of storage and were used. In a day when clergy were expected to be a bit aloof, this program time was the exception. And the same rules were relaxed for other adults.

Good news in 1947 came in several packages. Ten shares of Kimberly-Clark Preferred Stock with a market value of $1,100 were given to Kanuga by James C. Kimberly. Immediate needs dictated that this stock be sold and the money applied to decrease Kanuga's indebtedness. James Kimberly was a generous supporter of the Episcopal church in general and came to know Kanuga through his many visits to Tryon where his father, sister, and brother all had homes. At this same time the Rev. B. Duvall Chambers gave Kanuga government bonds in the amount of $200. The Kanuga Association had $3,607 in the bank and had new pledges of $1,340. The board also in 1947 decided that Kanuga should operate its own bookstore. The store operator would have entire supervision of the store and in return for this duty would receive room and board and 50 percent of the net proceeds. There had in the past been complaints that teachers and others who would need religious literature would not readily cooperate in meeting ordering deadlines and material would arrive late. The proposed bookstore would also possibly render a bit of profit.

The single greatest revenue producer was and long had been the Boys' Camp. Director of the camp, Ted Bost, at this same time asked for an appropriation of $200 to cover the cost of constructing and equipping a rifle range at the camp. After much discussion—and with a dissenting vote—the request was approved. A contemporary recruiting brochure of "Kanuga Camp for Boys" states that the camp is "in essence, a Church Camp owned by, and located upon the grounds of the Episcopal Church Conference Center. However, boys from all faiths are accepted." There is a picture of Kirk Arms, a large rustic cabin with a porch which "houses the screened-in-mess hall and kitchen, Trading Post, and Camp Office, with woodworking machine shop and craft shops underneath." There is a picture of six cabins which are "equipped with double-decker bunks, and contain either one or two leaders." Three tennis courts are pictured and a rifle range is shown with prone boys on the firing line. The caption identifies marksmanship practice as "probably the most popular activity." Also there is a picture of an archery line-up and a picture of the Council Ring, with the "stone Altar that was erected by campers in 1947," and that "is used for Evening Vespers and the Sunday Morning Service." The camp after 1947 was limited to Episcopal Church boys until June 1 and after that date boys of other churches were admitted until the camp quota was reached.

At the July 1947 meeting, Mrs. A. B. Stoney of Morganton, North Carolina, presented to Kanuga a new classroom as a memorial to Dr. Maurice Clarke. (The Clarke memorial brings the number of classrooms to five.) Dr. Clarke had for eleven years prior to his 1947 death been rector of Grace Church, Camden, and had represented the Diocese of Upper South Carolina on the Board of Managers. The Episcopal Church in South Carolina characterized him as having "attained much distinction especially in the field of religious education." Bishop Jackson was honored at this meeting for his eighteen years as director of the Adult Conference. He was described by Bishop Gravatt as a "continuing link with Bishop Finlay." Bishop Jackson died in New Orleans in 1948.

In July 1948, a long-standing road problem was partly solved when an agreement was reached with Col. J. C. Smoot in which

Kanuga would relinquish 16 acres of land in exchange for right-of-way access across some of his property to provide the re-routing, which actually straightened the road entering from the paved road at Drake's Store. Drake's Store stood near the place where the Kanuga triangular sign now stands.

Bishop Middleton S. Barnwell of the Diocese of Georgia asked the board if it would be possible for his diocese to build "The Georgia House" on Kanuga property which people of his diocese might use when at Kanuga. Pinckney raised the question of the possible sale or lease of land for private home sites, a long unresolved question. Mrs. Finlay occupied a cottage on the property at her pleasure and Cottage #2 was set aside for any bishop who would come and occupy that cottage for as much of the summer season as possible. Obviously, no clear purpose for land use and for future housing had begun to take shape. Each such question in the past had been resolved by what seemed to be self-evident to people of good will. At this same time, William S. Lea, who had been dean of the 1948 Adult Conference, had written the board asking, "after a conference with Bishop Dandridge (Edmund P. Dandridge), if the Diocese of Tennessee might not come into the Kanuga family on the same basis as did the Diocese of Louisiana, for the convenience especially of the Eastern Tennessee part of the state, making Tennessee 'an affiliated Diocese with one board representative.'" The matter was referred to the Executive Committee. There is no record of a formal reply either to the Georgia diocesan request or to the more formal Tennessee diocesan request. Some correspondence in the years following does include Tennessee as a participating diocese.

A four-page document, dated August 21, 1947, and signed by thirteen "annual guests" very critical of health and safety factors at Kanuga, was that fall finding its way throughout the dioceses which supported Kanuga. Walter Grace, who had several years earlier provided a study of Kanuga needs, was signatory of the letter as well as several other long-time Kanuga supporters. The report began with a property analysis which stated that they believed some 600,000 feet of good timber averaging from $35.00 to $50.00 per thousand feet now could be harvested for profit and that if not so harvested would deteriorate in quality and conse-quently devalue. They enumerated the problems they saw and accordingly set forth a financial solution for the problems they would solve. The letter also addressed the question of Kanuga liability when bad things happen as a result of this neglect. Board minutes January 27, 1948, summarized the complaints in the document as: grease traps not working, grease spilling out above ground being offensive, outside wiring obviously in need of repair, split lead water pipes above the dining room overflowing and the water coming through the ceiling, and major plumbing problems existing in Annexes A, B, C, and D, and in the Inn. This letter was much more than a statement of concerns; the drafters of the letter asked that Kanuga be immediately closed until health and safety conditions were satisfactory.

The Executive Committee meeting in Trinity Parish House, Columbia, September 30, 1948, addressed that question of the round-robin letter. While it cannot be stated that their actions were in direct response to the letter, the actions were responding to conditions enumerated in the letter. The committee asked the trustees to secure a five-year loan of $30,000, with Kanuga property to be mortgaged if necessary, to pay the $23,250 indebtedness then secured by notes against Kanuga. The balance remaining would provide operating expenses until June 1949, when income from the summer program would become available. Some needed repairs would then be made from the available operating expense account. There would also be cost-saving administrative controls put in place so that in all matters of policy regarding summer programs the superintendent should be consulted and his decisions followed. This administrative measure was designed to curtail staff decisions which had incurred labor costs.

At the meeting of the Board of Managers the following day, the board authorized borrowing up to $30,000, and gave approval to the idea of a fund-raising campaign. No action, however, was taken to implement the fund-raising suggestion. R. F. Huneycutt was again elected as caretaker although he had requested that the board accept his resignation. The board would not accept his resignation and asked the secretary to write to him and assure him that he was more than ever necessary to Kanuga. One of the board members referred to him as "Mr. Kanuga."

The Kanuga junior-college idea that had been nourished by some for a very long time was laid to rest in 1949, but it was not a silent departure. *The Asheville Citizen*, April 17, 1949, ran a page-one story about the new Finlay Junior College which would officially open July 23 quoting the Rev. John A. Pinckney who had prepared the lengthy news release. Other papers in the state picked up the story. The following day the papers carried a retraction of the story quoting Kanuga president Bishop Gravatt who denied that plans were even being considered for the development of such an institution. He said that the story apparently grew out of plans to give courses for college credits to Kanuga staff members. At the February 1949 board meeting Bishop Gravatt closed the chapter on the school when he said "there seems to be no particular need" in this area for this kind of school.

Western North Carolina's new bishop, the Rt. Rev. George Henry, was elected president of the association at the November 1949 meeting. Bishop Henry marked a transition in Kanuga's leadership from the devoted admirers who had known and worked with Bishop Finlay to one who as a young minister had on a few occasions met the man. The very real financial plight of Kanuga was very much on the agenda of the board. William L. Balthis, a lay board member, got agreement that the Committee on Finance and the Committee for Long-Range Planning would meet together (as the idea developed with the full board) and come to agreement on a way to deal with these financial problems.

The following December an agreement was reached within the Board of Managers for a 15 percent rate increase for all camps and conferences the following summer. The board discussed the question of a general campaign and felt it would be unwise at this time. The board recommended that each diocese place Kanuga in its budget and that a Kanuga Easter offering be taken in each diocese. The superintendent and all board members should "solicit in a quiet way funds...for the establishment of an endowment."

John A. Pinckney, having continued since 1943 on a year-to-year appointment as Kanuga superintendent, in his 1949 end-of-the-year report to the board stated:

> Looking at the overall picture and program of Kanuga, many people this past season expressed grave concern as to her future. Among those so concerned were some who have been at Kanuga since the beginning.... This past summer many patrons wondered just how much longer Kanuga would continue to attract people if we did not paint and repair the interior of the buildings and replace much furniture.

Chapter Six
The Fifties

Everything must be done to secure Kanuga's future. There should never be any conflict between Kanuga and any diocesan camp, no matter where they are located. Yet at the same time there is a growing interest in diocesan camps, which I fear will greatly handicap and retard the overall Kanuga program, although there is no necessity [for this to happen].[1]

The Rev. John A. Pinckney

In measuring Kanuga's success, the number of persons enrolled and attending a Kanuga conference is one important ingredient. The other measure, of course, is the quality of the Kanuga experience. If any one thing comes through to those reading the Kanuga minutes it is the concern with the quality of the Kanuga program. This is reinforced when one reads the personal correspondence of the bishops as they make comments on selecting and evaluating the speakers, teachers, and conference directors. This evaluation also was formalized in a study of the curriculum both in 1949 and in 1950.

The 1950 study group reported: "The Curriculum Committee is delighted that the conference directors so heartily approve of their 1949 recommendations and carried so many of them out in detail. The courses were well organized, the faculty good, and all of the conferences were, on the whole, most satisfactory to those who attended. Most favorable comments were made on the Adult Conference!"

The same committee recommended "that the schedule be synchronized with the schedules of the Provincial conferences and the various Diocesan Camp conferences.... The Kanuga program should be an integrated whole and should be part of the total Provincial Religious Educational Program.... The faculty should be rotated at least every three years to provide more variety and stimulation."

The other part of the equation—attendance—was in the late '40s and early '50s not so good. Excluding the Guest Period and counselors, the attendance in 1949 was 763 and in 1950 was 732. The low would be reached in 1951 when attendance was 666. And since registrations foretell to a considerable degree the forthcoming attendance, all through 1950 the board was working with gloomy forecasts. The Guest Period was important financially, yet there was a concern that while offering church families a vacation in a Christian atmosphere, this aspect of Kanuga was not sufficiently part of the defined Christian education program that Kanuga was set up to be. The arithmetic does not include counselors as those served by Kanuga, yet it was recognized at an early date that the counselors and other young people who worked at the conferences frequently were the ones who derived the most significance from a Kanuga conference.

When the Board of Managers met early in January 1950, at the Church of the Good Shepherd in Raleigh, two major agenda items were on their minds although the agenda was long. First was the proposed Easter offering for Kanuga held in the supporting dioceses. The board president would write to each bishop and make this a formal request. To put this into perspective, bishops would be asked to place Kanuga alongside the many other diocesan institutions also asking for funding. Second on their minds at this meeting was the selection process they were about to begin to find a full-time year-round general manager. The Executive Committee was empowered to proceed to engage the services of such a manager subject to final approval by the board.

At this same meeting the Kanuga board acted to accept the work that had been under way for some time to file a certificate of incorporation under North Carolina law. From the time the round-robin letter had alerted the board's attention to the law concerning negligence and liability there was concern that this matter be cleared up. When the Kanuga Conferences Association was formed little attention had been given to this, partly because of the complicated way the financial package was put together.

(George Stephens and Bishop Finlay underwrote the arrangement with their $8,500 equity to be resolved at some future date.)
That was 1928 and papers of incorporation were not seen as
necessary if even possible at that time. But immediately after the
1947 question of ownership liability was raised, the corrective
remedial legal work was begun. Each diocesan convention would
have to approve articles of incorporation—so it was a process
which would take some time.

The Executive Committee met in Columbia soon after the
board meeting with the purpose "being the matter of employing a
full-time Superintendent and Director of Kanuga." His duties
were defined as "resident manager, manager of camps and
conferences, in charge of promotion, bursar, and employer of all
necessary help." His salary was open and he must be an Episcopalian. A search process began immediately and several names
emerged with a final list of five which was then reduced to one.

At a called meeting of the Board of Managers, Willard P.
("Bill") Verduin was employed as general manager with a yearly
salary of $3,600 plus house and electricity, meals for all his family
in the dining room during the conference season, and $600 for
promotional travel. His Georgetown, South Carolina, rector, the
Rev. H. D. Bull, described Bill as faithful in his church attendance,
working in the church school, and with his wife Evelyn, attending
confirmation class. The "handsome couple, courteous, quiet,
good-tempered" also had a five-year-old daughter, Elizabeth
Terry, he added. Verduin was a graduate of the University of
Michigan and was employed at the West Virginia Pulp and Paper
Company which at that time had large holdings in the Georgetown
area.

As Bishop George Henry's election as board president marked
a departure from the Bishop Finlay experience, so did the
selection of Bill Verduin. While Verduin was being considered
along with four others by the executive committee, superintendent Pinckney recognized this evolving change in Kanuga leadership and cautioned Bishop Henry: "Very few laymen have had the
insight into Kanuga...and the ramifications of camps and
conferences...[which would enable] the idea established long ago
[to be] carried on."

Verduin spent the summer of 1950 at Kanuga observing the
operation and then officially came aboard September 1, 1950, at

the conclusion of the summer conference season. When asked forty-three years later why he took the job, he replied, "I was overwhelmed by the magnitude of the challenge—partly because of the wretched condition of the physical plant." He added: "There were no crutches to lean on. Records hardly existed. Bishop Henry was kind to me but he was a very busy man. It was my baby, to sink or swim." An interesting "Dear George" letter from "Capers" in November lets Bishop George Henry know the attitude of Spartanburg Church of the Advent rector, Capers Satterlee, towards the new manager. "First of all, I like the man's attitude and the way he talked.... Regardless of money made or lost by the adult conference, our first obligation is to house the staff in as adequate quarters as possible, so that we are not at least asking for trouble.... I was delighted that Verduin said it before I did, for that means he was not at all pushed into it." The subject was finding a satisfactory lounge room for the staff.[2]

The Boys' Camp was not operating in 1950 since there had been only four registrations. The Young People's Conference was, for the fifth year, a financial disappointment. The Easter offering possibly would bring in $11,000, the board was told. Overall they would conclude the season with a cash balance of about $5,000. But there was a sobering reminder, "that the water system is 40 years old, and will have to be replaced in the not far distant future."

The board minutes of November 14, 1950, recognize that Kanuga Articles of Incorporation had been filed on July 26, 1950, in the Office of the Clerk of the Court, Hendersonville, in book 4, page 191. The minutes of that meeting read "First Regular Meeting of Kanuga Conferences, Inc. held at St. Martin's Church, Charlotte, N.C." This also was the first meeting of the Board of Managers that Verduin attended. The four legal-sized pages of minutes were the most extensive minutes of the board until that time. It was a full agenda and was mixed with emotion when an inscribed watch was presented to Mr. Pinckney. He had been in leadership at Kanuga since 1932. Mr. Huneycutt's service to Kanuga as property manager for over forty years was recognized and F. D. MacLean's long service as treasurer was also recognized in the same press release which had been prepared to announce the appointment of the new general manager (Bill Verduin).

Necessary details filled much of the meeting. New Kanuga

by-laws were passed to conform to the new articles of incorporation; conference dates were set; the Boys' Camp would be reinstituted; and then the board discussed the importance of Kanuga sending out their conference schedule early so that diocesan conferences could avoid conflict with Kanuga dates.

Gastonia layman and board member William L. Balthis' remarks are recorded in the minutes as follows:

> *that the physical properties call for a lot of money being expended on them...a minimum of $139,000 would just cover the cost of necessary improvements, and...that we should set a goal of $250,000. He asked if the bishops would approve a campaign to raise this amount, $250,000, which he considered absolutely necessary. He suggested that such an endeavor be called "The Kanuga Foundation."*

There was hesitation. One bishop spoke of other very necessary diocesan campaigns in the offing. Another board member stated that a land tract sale would raise a lot of money. The Easter campaign just completed had raised only $8,425 and not the ten thousand-plus that had been expected.

Bishop Henry resolved the matter by asking Balthis to select a committee that would consult with all the diocesan bishops and said that he believed that the strength of the people who would be elected for the committee would bring the bishops around to supporting the campaign. The committee was composed of Bishop Gravatt of the Diocese of Upper South Carolina, board members Ernest Patton, James Gary, and W. L. Mauney of Asheville, Mrs. Francis E. Field of Biltmore Forest, Asheville, and John W. Arrington III, of Greenville, South Carolina.

In a personal letter to Balthis soon after the meeting, Bishop Gravatt provided his perspective on the past fund-raising efforts. He said he did not think there would be a problem in securing the consent of the diocesan bishops but told Balthis that he should be aware of problems that campaigns in the past had encountered:

> *John M. Rivers of Charleston in 1946 became interested in raising money for Kanuga because he felt that the Boys' Camp should be decidedly improved.... This campaign largely failed, I think, because it was simply a letter approach.... Mr. Rivers gave his $1,000 and raised a little more, but that was all.... A 1948 urge for money raising that came chiefly from some of the*

laymen present at the Guest Period failed, I think, because we lacked a contact man.... Pinckney agreed to go but it never seemed to work out.... He never seemed to be able to get to the places and see the members of the committees that he had requested by mail to serve.... Mr. Verduin...can go to chosen places, see certain individuals and through personal contact get them interested in the canvass, [and] I believe we can accomplish much.

At the October 1951 Board of Managers meeting, Balthis presented a report of his committee on funds needed for repair and asked the board's approval of a campaign for $150,000, a sum the committee had decided was easier to raise than the $250,000 Balthis had earlier said was necessary. The sum would be $3.50 for each communicant in the owning dioceses. Bishop Henry asked that the figure be revised to $3.75 per communicant "since it might not be fair to include the colored communicants since they do not benefit from Kanuga." The telling board action on this campaign that had gotten off to such an enthusiastic start was that the board adopted a motion that each diocese would handle the method of running the campaign in each respective diocese. In effect there would be no organized campaign; again, there would be a Kanuga offering, taken at some time, in some parishes.

Verduin began a newsletter his first year which he sent out to a mailing list of 1,600. It was called *The Bugle*. The purpose of the mimeographed newsy letter was to inform and to generate interest in the coming Kanuga season. The spring edition thanked those who had responded to the new communication, stating they "were completely unprepared for the number of replies it brought forth." There were comments about all the scheduled conferences: "Looks as though we might have very near capacity crowd for most groups." And about the Guest Period, *The Bugle* implored: "If you don't have a family, come and be part of the Kanuga family. There just isn't such a thing as loneliness or boredom at Kanuga." The readers were told, "the Boys' Camp will be in full swing again this year," with Freeman Self, a former Boy Scout executive, in charge.

Betsy Campbell of Gaffney, South Carolina, once wrote about Mr. Verduin: "I remember him best for his beautiful dahlia garden [Bill Verduin continued this garden originally started by Rufus Morgan] and the superb young people he had on his staff."

Also she has provided us with a delightfully written account of the beginning efforts at Kanuga towards serious religious education for young children.

> *The beginning of Kanuga's strong children's program came about 1950. Up until that time, two ladies would "keep" children during the two week period of Adult Conference. The 1950 conference brought more children than the ladies could possibly handle. The Rev. Skardon D'Aubert of Houston, Texas, had come for the Adult Conference. He saw the situation with the children and offered to help. He had a magnetism that children responded to the minute they met him. They followed him as if he was the "Pied Piper of Hamelin."*

> *What he told the children to do, they did. What he told them not to do, they didn't. He told them Bible stories and he told the old-time fairy stories of Andersen and Grimm and they hung on his every word. Each night during Vespers, he loaded them on the ark, sailed them as far from where the service was taking place as possible and led them in songs such as "There Were Three Jolly Fishermen."*

> *Starting with 1951, Father D'Aubert organized a "Children's Mission" to be conducted during Adult Conference. He expanded on the things he had done in 1950. He got a few helpers together. The children ate lunch and dinner with him. By the Grace of God, they learned table manners from Father D'Aubert. At that time there was a small altar in the left transept of the Chapel. He took the children in there for services every day. They learned simple prayers and simple hymns. He took them on hikes and with his helpers supervised their swimming.*

> *There was always a banquet the last night of Adult Conference. In their small dining area the children had a banquet too. They had appropriate decorations, appropriate prayers, speeches and songs. Father D'Aubert conducted this Children's Mission for about five years. It was wonderful!* [3]

In the summer of 1952, two new conferences were introduced. One, "Leadership Training Conference for Youth," was Kanuga's response to the previous year's fifth consecutive decline in attendance at the Young People's Conference. The growth of diocesan youth conferences was the reason for the decline. Kanuga would then train leaders for those diocesan conferences. The other conference broke new ground. It was "An Experiment in Christian Family Living" and was led by the Rev. C. Alfred Cole of St. John's, Charleston, West Virginia. The entire program was geared to include every member of the family working, worshipping, studying, and playing together. Toddlers, grandparents, and every age group in between were participants. "As far as any record can be found this was the first conference along these definite family lines attempted at a regular conference center in any Episcopal church center," Frank Ballard stated in his unpublished Kanuga history in 1978.

Kanuga conference attendance in 1952 was 792; in 1953, it was 968; and, in 1954, was 1,197. The leadership training conference more than doubled from 40 the first year to 108 in 1954; and the family conference held its own, 122 the first year and 128 in 1954. In 1953, there was a new Conference on Parish Schools that grew from 32 the first year to 87 the next. Something was working. Kanuga's leadership was identifying a need; and by defining it in relationship to Kanuga's capabilities, it was answering that need.

By 1954, Kanuga was suffering from growing pains. The crop of "war babies" was reaching camp age and the camping program for young people more than doubled. Four new conferences for teenagers and adults were added and plans were afoot to add three more in 1955. The conferences "were filling very real needs in the life of the Church hitherto neglected," a report on capital funds stated. The 1954 report also spoke of the necessity of purchasing a large number of new beds and the need for facilities for faculty and staff at the camp and for a resident maintenance man.

The old hotel continued to be the center of Kanuga activities. With its four annexes, the hotel could sleep sixty-four in each. Some rooms had private baths but the occupants of most of the rooms shared a common bath which was not an uncommon arrangement in 1909 hotel design. Bishop Robert W. Estill recalls one time "immersing myself in a tub of hot water, only to discover that I was sharing the bathroom with two ladies who had failed to lock 'my side' of the door." The rooms all had been furnished for family use, which meant double beds. Kanuga's conference hotel occupants not only shared a room, they shared a common bed. Verduin early began to put twin beds in the rooms and began to clean up the old property. Rooms were painted, some two-hundred cracked or broken window panes were replaced, and new exterior stain was applied to the cottages. The repairs in the children's dining room were none too soon. Only one day after the conclusion of a conference, one-fourth of the ceiling collapsed. One old slot machine from Kanuga's last days as a private resort was found about this time also.

Adults ate in the large dining room and children and very young children—some who were accompanied by family maids— ate in the children's dining room. The old hotel was designed so children and adults would dine separately. Some families especially from Columbia and from Charleston continued into the 1950s to come to Kanuga with maids who took care of their children. Some who came also expected to have the fish, caught during recreation time, individually prepared for them and served instead of the regular hotel fare. Printed instructions to guests at an Adult Conference contained the admonishment, "Please do not ask the kitchen or dining room hostess for tray service or coffee to be taken out of the dining room."

It was about this same time that a woman from the eastern part of the state wrote to make an adult conference reservation requesting a private bath. The policy—in the interest of simplicity and fairness—was to assign rooms at random with the private bath being a bit of luck. She was insistent and the busy Kanuga manager sent her a letter that on reflection was more terse than he had wished. Fortunately, he had used the wrong address, the letter was returned, and he by then was able to assure private accommodations. Mrs. Fannie Grist Staton thoroughly enjoyed the conference. She died a year later and left $40,000 in her will for Kanuga. The Board of Managers earmarked this bequest for the construction of a new kitchen wing which would be the first part of a new administration wing, when and if that day would come.

Volume I, Number 1 of *Kanuga News* was published March 1957. This was lithograph printed, well-written, and well-edited. It did some recruiting; it told the readers that financial support from the Woman's Auxiliary was growing and during the last year had reached about $3,000. They were told: "Cub Camp this year would include boys finishing fourth grade and the program has been revised to accommodate this newer age span." Sadly, the first edition carried the news of the death of William Henry Kinckle Pendleton, 1867-1956. *Kanuga News* in March reported more new beds and mattresses and announced one promising innovation for the coming summer—the addition of Jack Arrington as chaplain to the staff. And the upbeat news continued when the October *Kanuga News* reported that just about 2,000 young people from ages 8-17 participated in camps and conferences in the Carolinas the past summer and about 700 of those had come to Kanuga. Also reported, was a two-day conference in September on church camps. The focus of the conference was (1) the place of camps and conferences in the Christian Education program of the church, and (2) the relationship between Kanuga and the other camps in the several owning dioceses.

"The Board of Managers has approved the preliminary plans and the architect is putting the final touches on the final draft.... We will have a new kitchen in service by next summer," the *Kanuga News* reported in October 1958. The county health inspector had for many years expressed his concern about the physical condition of the kitchen. He once told the director that if he did his duty, he would close the kitchen on the spot. In 1956, the board had secured a construction engineer's report on the old hotel building and was told that the old friend would ultimately have to be replaced. It was beyond redemption. "Since Kanuga can hardly expect to replace the entire structure at any one time, it seemed advisable to plan a new building that could be built in sections over the course of many years," the newsletter stated.

Planning the new kitchen was much more than designing an addition. The first job to be done was to plan in some detail the entire new building because the new kitchen would be part of the new structure and not just serve the present hotel dining rooms. The first wing of a new building that most probably would be constructed in sections over the course of many years, called for serious planning. Carolina Construction Company of Asheville was the low bidder at $47,800. It was estimated that, including certain needed equipment and the architect's fees, the total cost would run between $55,000 and $60,000.

Kanuga had, for about four years, been operating in the black—but just barely. There continued to be a laundry list of needed improvements, but growth was producing some income that could be used for capital improvements. A new $6,000 recreation building was under construction. The 30 x 80 foot structure would have a great fireplace on the back wall with a 20 x 30 foot classroom at either end of the building. Currently, the building is still the primary activity building for the Wildlife Camp which is located there now. This was a building that had been needed for thirty years. The room would accommodate all sorts of indoor recreation and rainy-day activities. Vespers could be held there when it was raining. Only those who have supervised young people at camp can appreciate what it is like not to have options for rainy-day activities. Also, out of this bit of growing revenue, four new rowboats were ordered to add to the fleet.

Bishop Henry had stepped down as board president in 1957. He was followed temporarily by Bishop C. Alfred Cole of the Diocese of Upper South Carolina and then by the Rev. Capers Satterlee of the same diocese. Bishops did not want the Kanuga responsibility. Bishop Thomas H. Wright of the East Carolina diocese declined the job stating that he had taken a solemn vow "to take on nothing new." Bishop Henry had once told his wife that he had been elected because in essence he was the new bishop in the club. While a reluctant acceptance of the job it may have been, his voluminous correspondence about Kanuga problems provides evidence that he did it with full dedication. In 1959, a portrait of Bishop Henry was offered to Kanuga in appreciation for his work there. July 13, 1959 minutes record: "The thinking of the present board is that there is, and should be, only one portrait at Kanuga—that of the founder, Bishop Finlay—and that the offer therefore be tactfully rejected."

While the physical growth of Kanuga can be described, the spiritual growth of the people who gathered there is recorded—if at all—years later. In the summer of 1957, the Adult Conference had scheduled two principal speakers. They were the dean of the School of Theology at The University of the South in Sewanee, George M. Alexander, and Ernest Southcutt of Southark, England, whose books on prayer had attracted much attention. Both of these headliners had a following. Two young priests, Jack Spong and Bob Estill, were slated to help with the accompanying seminars. Both of the celebrities had to cancel at the last minute. Many years later, the Rt. Rev. John Shelby Spong wrote: "The material I had already prepared for a small seminar became the major lectures at the conference. Each day that week, for the first time publicly, I shared my thoughts on the Resurrection. The response was enormously encouraging." Sitting in the library at Kanuga in 1993, he shared with this writer what he wrote in *The Easter Moment*, "That there are some high points in the pilgrimage," and one he said, "was at Kanuga that summer in 1957." The Rt. Rev. Robert W. Estill recalled the classes were conducted in the small buildings that are now called The Grove. "We did that [conferences with Spong] for six straight years—a record of sorts," he said.

Kanuga was growing. Finance committee chairman H. P. Duvall in a formal report to the board stated that: "The board looks with concern and alarm at the ever increasing number of people, especially children and teenagers, for whom there is no room at the Inn." He reviewed the financial structure of Kanuga and said that still there is no "clear, comprehensive statement of policy with respect to the financing of Kanuga." It was the same sentiment Verduin presented to the board when he said, "I don't want to sound rough or tough, but an old cliche fits appropriately at this time—Somebody's got to do something, even if it is wrong." Bishop Thomas A. Fraser, Jr., of the Diocese of North Carolina in another board meeting asked, "Who is responsible for Kanuga?" He stated that the only real hold Kanuga had on anyone was their love of Kanuga. He pointed out that this was a very nebulous responsibility that each diocese has or feels.

A full-time program director was added to the staff in the April 1961 appointment of Ed Hartley. Bishop Fraser reported that while he and the chairman were trying to draw up a job description they met Hartley and were impressed with his background in Y.M.C.A. work and accordingly employed him. Both Hartley and Verduin attended and participated at board meetings. The Executive Committee was directed to outline the duties assigned to each man. The board chairman continued to be consulted on almost any decision with copies of that correspondence sent to the bishops of the dioceses.

Kanuga Camp for Boys had been so named and the site, which was approved in the winter of 1960, had become operational in 1962. The sessions were called simply First Session and Second Session, with 12-day sessions accommodating about 60 boys at each session. T. Edmund Whitmore of Asheville was the project's architect. All of the cabins and the recreation center were cut from Kanuga timber. A small lake with ridgecrest backdrop was downhill from the cabins. It was named Lake McCready in honor of the donors, Mr. and Mrs. Stephen McCready of Ocala, Florida.

The first summer the camp was in use, the boys helped create an outdoor chapel. From a hill at one end of the lake the young chapel goers could see beyond the lake three mountains grouped in a natural Trinity. They named the path, from the chapel to the log bridge across a stream, "God's Walk" and called the stream "Silent Brook" and began what was to become a tradition that no word was to be spoken from the time one would leave the chapel until they crossed the bridge.

With the addition of the new Camp for Boys, Kanuga was now a three-fold operation—boys' camp, girls' camp, and the conference center. The summer of 1962, Kanuga hosted 475 young campers and 815 conferees in 12 conferences and a filled Guest Period. There was in 1962 a total of 85 buildings, some 21 of which were erected within the last ten years. Building number 86, a staff cabin at the Boys' Camp and building number 87, a staff cabin at Girls' Camp, were under construction that same summer. Underground and unobservable, there was now in place a sewer system that replaced septic tanks that never should have been put where they were in the first place—and there was hot water.

The Boys' Camp ran pretty heavily in the red the first year—$8,600. Verduin's recommendation to the board that the fees be raised from $55 to $65 per session and Hartley's opposition to the fee increase created an awkward vote to which the board was not accustomed. It passed. The board recognized that the absence of job definitions had caused the problem and the Executive Committee was asked to review the working relationship between the two staff members. Bishop Henry at an earlier board meeting had observed that a title for Hartley had never been decided on.

All through the life of Kanuga was the little-discussed question of integration. The only time the board had been required to vote in any way on the question of admitting black Episcopalians to Kanuga was in 1938. "After considerable discussion," the minutes report, "the board regrets that it cannot accede to the request of the troop of Boy Scouts of St. Matthais' Church, Asheville, to use Kanuga grounds for camping." "Bishop Finlay brought colored help up from South Carolina with him each summer to work at the hotel," Miss Lucy Fletcher tells us. How long into Bishop Finlay's tenure this practice continued is not known. Lucy Fletcher also tells us about "stunt nights—minstrels—black face for a few years, then Bishop Finlay stopped this." The black kitchen workers were housed at first in rooms under the old hotel kitchen. Later, in 1945, board minutes report "moving Negro quarters." Treasurer F. D. MacLean told Bishop Henry in a May 9, 1950 note that, "I guess John told you the Negro quarters are completed." This new building is the building now named Baker Building.

In September 1956, the Division of Camps and Conferences of the Province of Sewanee met to discuss the question of segregated camps and conferences in the province. The following October, a special Kanuga committee met to consider the same subject. The recommendation to "experiment" with permitting limited integration at the Woman's Auxiliary Conference was rejected because these were older women who were the least apt of all to accept the idea, the board reasoned. Rather, "the Clergy Conference should be open to Negroes and that an effort be made to get Negro clergy to attend." For several more years there were discussion and postponement.

The Rt. Rev. Albert R. Stuart, Bishop of Georgia, addressing the Synod of the Fourth Province in 1965 at Sewanee, provided a retrospective view of the intense feelings about these issues when he observed: "My term of office had been one during which our Province has had trying times. The social revolution going on about us has caused disunity among some of us. Some of our priests and some of our laity have separated themselves from us."

The specific Kanuga board action to define the Kanuga position on integration came in response to a request from the Diocese of North Carolina. In July 1963, the Kanuga board adopted a resolution in reply to the chairman of the Executive Council of that diocese, "that Kanuga announces its willingness to admit all qualified persons to its camps and conferences regardless of race."

ӘꓯᏕ

26. Chapel of the Transfiguration, built 1940, dedicated 1942.

27. Lych-gate, gift of the Rev. Duvall Chambers and his wife Mary, from Columbia, South Carolina.

28. Chapel interior prior to 1977 alterations.

29. Lakeside Chapel, before 1987 renovation.

30.   Chapel of St. Francis of Assissi with 1942 Penland School of Handicrafts' fired-clay frontal.

31.　Kirk Arms Hall, 1947, Kanuga Camp for Boys.
(Photograph courtesy Baker-Barber Collection, Hendersonville)

32.　Archery, 1947, Kanuga Camp for Boys.
(Photograph courtesy Baker-Barber Collection, Hendersonville)

33. Girls' camping session, 1963, West Camp.
(Edward L. DuPuy Photography, Black Mountain)

34. Boys' camping session, 1963, new camp location for boys.
(Edward L. DuPuy Photography, Black Mountain)

35. Launching 1965 development program. From left: Bert King, the Rev. John W. Arrington III, the Rt. Rev. John A. Pinckney, property committee chairman Don M. White, Jr.

(Putnam Photography, Asheville)

36. Ground-breaking for new Kanuga Inn, 1967. Right to left: John Arrington III, chairman of Kanuga Board of Directors; the Rt. Rev. George Henry, bishop of Western North Carolina; Clyde Jackson, chairman, Hendersonville Board of Commissioners; Melvin S. Hatch, Mayor pro tem, city of Hendersonville; Edgar Hartley, Jr., executive director, Kanuga; not identified.

37. Construction, 1968.

38. Construction, 1968.

39. New Kanuga Lake Inn dedicated. June 30, 1968.

Chapter Seven
Building Years

*Bishop Henry said that he didn't know how many
committees had been appointed to study long-range
planning in the last 15 years, but nothing had come of
them. We do need a new dining hall and more adequate
office space. It is time to make up our minds on that. If we
need the dining halls replaced and more adequate office
space, let's do something about it.*[1]

Minutes, Board of Managers, July 8, 1963

No period of Kanuga's history is characterized by so much
ambiguity as the first part of the decade of the 1960s. Attendance
at conferences—what Kanuga was all about—had never been so
high. Financial support was averaging $10,000 for each diocese
and growing with the money coming from parishes and the
churchwomen's organizations. Debts were paid and the growing
camp and conference income, coupled with the judicious management of Kanuga's thousand and more acres of forest, had
permitted, in the past decade, improvements of a quarter of a
million dollars. Although Kanuga paid taxes of $10 per acre on
this income-producing land, its harvest was productive and with
replanting meant either possible income for the future or preservation of forest land that never again could the church possibly
hope to have.

It was increasingly evident that Kanuga was on the verge of
a massive expansion of facilities and nothing was really going to
hold it back. The only question was—what and when will it
happen? And will it be wisely done? In the summer of 1963,
architect Bertram King had been employed by the executive

committee to present some drawings of a proposed building to replace the old hotel. The committee had met with two hotel men and a banker which suggested to some that only replacement of the building inherited from the past was being considered.

The preliminary sketch or "rendering" of a possible building immediately brought inquiries to the board. A North Carolina diocesan executive committee member presented a proposed format to review the whole Kanuga enterprise even to asking, "Has the board ever considered use of Kanuga for something quite different, such as a boys' school?" Diocesan of North Carolina, Bishop Fraser, resigned as vice-president of the board, saying that he did not have time to give to such a program. Bishop Wright of the Diocese of East Carolina thought a committee should be appointed composed of the chairman of the Christian Education committee of each diocese and others who were interested to discuss Kanuga's future needs. Bishop Gray Temple of the Diocese of South Carolina "favored the idea of a committee to do some long range planning so as to have unanimity of opinion in the dioceses." Bill Verduin said he believed conclusions had been drawn without asking enough questions and without finding out some facts. Several board members asked why a committee could not meet with the diocesan departments of Christian Education. At long last the vote was called on the motion which had prompted the discussion:

> ...that the Board approve the action of the last meeting of the Executive Committee, the plan to replace the buildings with the raising of $500,000 for the necessary capital expenditures. [The motion passed.]

Mr. Willard Verduin resigned as Kanuga's general manager, September 1, 1963. He accepted a job at Camp Sequoia north of Asheville near Weaverville. The board in October recognized his "fine, conscientious work...and amazing results." He also was presented with a farewell check for $1,000.

Edgar Hartley was appointed acting executive director until such time as the board might secure a full-time person for this job, generally considered a position to be filled by a clergyman. Hartley was a Guilford College graduate and had some graduate work at Southern Methodist University. He was a retired Marine Corps Reserve major and had been in the life insurance business for thirteen years before coming to Kanuga.

Hartley served about a year and a half as acting director. One of his first interests was a revision of the Kanuga Foundation.[2] At his first meeting with the board he received the nod to begin this. At this same meeting the board agreed to review Kanuga's "total program" and asked a previous Kanuga superintendent and now the new bishop of the Diocese of Upper South Carolina, John Pinckney, to head this evaluation. The discussion by the board just prior to forming this committee made it clear that Kanuga could not be limited to an extension of the departments of Christian Education throughout the several dioceses, but that Kanuga now was an extension of the total programs of the several dioceses. How this emerging role affected all aspects of Kanuga was the task of the special committee to define.

The many-page document this committee produced, "Report of the Special Committee Appointed to Study Kanuga Conferences," was written principally by John S. Spong, and carries his name first, along with E. B. Jeffress, Joseph Horn, Mrs. Robert Haden (Mary Haden), and John Pinckney. While it is speculative whether a study committee document serves to shape future decisions or makes more plausible and understandable the decisions that must be made, the document produced by this committee was the most comprehensive and thoughtful Kanuga had had to date:

No one assumes direct responsibility...authority vacuum...no real competition with diocesan camps...for some a sort of spiritual fun spot for old Carolina Episcopalians...rather clannish spirit among those who return year after year...greatest need with camps is adequate long-range leadership...the Adult Conference occupies a special place in the hearts and minds that for many is Kanuga...faculties in recent years featuring Dean George Alexander, Mrs. Samuel M. Shoemaker, Dr. FitzSimons Allison, Bishop Stephen Bayne, and Mrs. Gertrude Behanna fulfill all expectations in their presented courses...Mrs. Robert Dargan's drama group adds a new dimension to the entire program...the Young People's Conference is the only popular rival to the Adult Conference...it is too important to jeopardize by a decentralization back to the diocesan movement...in any future building the charm of this place should be kept...food just isn't what it used to be...not sell or lease any property...cost-wise a two-story building is a must...a veranda-type porch, facing the lake, should definitely be included...Kanuga needs two executives...must have an executive director...Kanuga can be presented in such a way as to tax the physical plant beyond capacity. [The report was accepted March 10, 1964, and the Executive Committee began to secure the services of an executive director.][3]

A special called two-day meeting of the board, in July 1964, met with the director of the Episcopal Church's National Council of Camps and Conferences, George Woodgate. The board took a tour of the property and reviewed both the plant and the programs. Hartley told them that the three-story section of the old hotel building must go after another summer and the only question was whether to replace just the three-story part or the whole building, exclusive of the kitchen. Hartley also outlined a plan for financing the construction through the issuance of a six-percent bond and a concerted promotion of annual giving by friends of Kanuga. It was possible, Hartley told them, that if approached this way, this plan would not have to be approved by the conventions of the five owning dioceses.

The December 1964 board meeting at Christ Church, Charlotte, was an action meeting. The board chairman introduced the newly-selected executive director, the Rev. John C. Grainger. He would begin work February 1, 1965. He was for fifteen years the rector of the Church of the Good Shepherd, Ruxton, Maryland. A Chapel Hill and Virginia Seminary graduate, Grainger had served parishes in Lincolnton and Shelby, North Carolina, and had two years of service as chaplain during World War II, He had been married in the Kanuga chapel to Emily Clarkson Ball and they had three sons, Cameron, Charles, and Heyward. He often was at Kanuga in the summers both attending and participating in conferences. He was popular in organizing evening entertainment programs and had learned about the position when he was at Kanuga the previous summer. There was in place a job description which he and board chairman, the Rev. Capers Satterlee, had worked out. His responsibilities in the forthcoming fund-raising campaign were included in this description. Ed Hartley would be named assistant director rather than business manager.

The forthcoming fund-raising campaign was the agenda throughout all board meetings in 1965. Conferences were going well. Hartley was getting a bookkeeping system in operation that would provide a monthly accounting of Kanuga finances. The new executive director was concerned about Kanuga's relationship with the diocesan education committees he had just visited, although this concern was not shared by the board. The dam required extensive repair and the offices were being planned under the chapel. The Executive Board of the Episcopal Church-women of the Diocese of Upper South Carolina was on record disapproving tearing down the old hotel and wanted it renovated and fire-proofed instead.

That a campaign had been approved was announced in December 1965. The National Fund-Raising Services, Inc., was employed to direct the campaign that would raise over a ten-year period five million dollars, beginning with an intensive campaign to raise one million dollars by May 30, 1966, as the initial first target date. Each of the bishops was on record supporting the goal, although three said they would do no personal soliciting and one cautioned that there were at that time seven campaigns in his diocese. Each, however, would give a supporting statement for publicity which would be used in the campaign. A Committee of 100 would be formed with fifteen business executives from each of the five dioceses, and three clergy from each diocese appointed by the separate bishops. The board was told that in a campaign of this kind, 40 percent of the goal could be expected to come from ten gifts.

The campaign was organized and the new board chairman, the Rev. John Arrington of Clemson, would serve as campaign chairman. Arrington was elected board chairman when Mr. Satterlee retired from the board at the onset of the campaign, November 1965. Arrington previously had been finance commit-tee chairman and was actively interested in Kanuga. Special stationery was printed with "$1,000,000 Development of Kanuga Conferences" as the letterhead. The *Kanuga News* had a new and more professional format. The first phase of the campaign was making and developing friends—friend raising, the professionals named it. Testimonials from old Kanuga friends were printed in a special *Kanuga News* that also announced the proposed new buildings. Pictured were the architectural drawings of three major buildings: (1) the lounge with its dramatic cathedral ceiling and fireplace; (2) the new main building complex that encompassed the bedroom area; and, (3) a lakefront recreational building designed to replace in time the pavilion and to be used for dramatic and social activities.

Spring and summer 1966 saw the campaign in action. The office was in the back bedroom of Cottage #8, then in the living room of Cottage #26. There were two telephones. "It was just Ed and a part-time bookkeeper and I, plus the maintenance staff. Until summer that was it. Later on, we got a secretary," Mary Hartley recalled for *Kanuga News* years later. She also described a day at Kanuga: "I would open the desk and greet the people and then run in the dining room and host there and then run to the canteen, and so on. It was like a Lucille Ball movie."

The manual developed for the campaign by the National Fund-Raising Services detailed both strategy and tactics. It was not scheming; it was action-planned with individuals chosen who would work raising money for Kanuga. First recorded reports of the campaign are found in the Executive Committee minutes, September 21, 1966. The reports were spotty. In Charleston, Y. W. Scarborough had between 50 and 60 people actively engaged in the campaign; William Bryan in Columbia had about 20 major gift prospects and about 80 special givers with an expectancy of doubling this. William K. Stephenson in Greenville was on target; Spartanburg had as yet no one in charge. Emsley A. Laney in Wilmington, and Manley W. Wright of Asheville, were at work. Winston-Salem, Charlotte, and the Goldsboro-Kinston area were without leaders. The board and area solicitation had yielded $102,700 with the possibility of that going higher. Hartley pointed out that the delay in securing manpower was due to the bishops not supplying names of chairmen and sub-chairmen, although he phrased the observation in more polite words.

The reaction to the contrast between the old Kanuga way of requesting a donation and a professional campaign was not always welcomed. "I was and am shocked, appalled, and dismayed, to use a few adjectives, at your approach to this fund drive," wrote one Asheville executive. He was offended by the "fancy brochure" with his name on it, and informed the committee that he and his wife were pledging only one-half of what had been requested.

Even with some areas of the two Carolinas not accounted for, there was at Kanuga toward the end of the summer season in 1966 the acceptance of the end of the era many had known. A story in an Asheville newspaper captures the sentiment of the last evening at the old hotel:

*Attorney Joseph Cumming's sentimental remarks interrupted
an amateur talent show, the last event ever to be held in
Kanuga's main building.... Rising from his seat in the sparse
audience composed of Kanuga's end-of-season guests and
cottagers, Cumming asked the master of ceremonies for per-
mission to say a few words.... "I first stood under this rotunda
almost 60 years ago when the building we are in was an
exclusive club and the room we are in was a gambling place....
Season after season, we and our children and grandchildren
have performed and sung together in these little entertainment
programs.... As a tribute to this old building and to our final
gathering within its walls, I propose that we sing 'Auld Lang
Syne.'"* [4]

In the midst of the campaign, executive director Grainger
and the board concluded that the management of Kanuga was
more business and less pastoral than they had realized it would
be and the board accepted his resignation, effective November
1966. Grainger accepted a call to become rector of St. Paul's
Episcopal Church in Petersburg, Virginia. Hartley was named
executive director of Kanuga at the board meeting the next day.
The development fund report was mixed news. Hartley optimis-
tically reported that he thought the Charleston experience indi-
cated that each of the ten areas divided for fund-raising would
meet the figure of $60,000. Charlotte and Raleigh were without
chairmen still but the campaign was now getting started in East
Carolina. Attorney Francis M. Coiner who had been invited to the
meeting answered questions of liability under law if Kanuga
should borrow money to begin building and then default on
payment. He alleviated their personal fears and added the further
advice that should the board wait another six months the building
costs would increase by six percent. He recommended they go
ahead and borrow and begin to build.

Stephenson observed that there was general agreement that
if the contract was not signed, the campaign would fail. Bishop
Pinckney said that the board should sign the contract "with faith
and action, or to take the necessary steps to dissolve the corporation and sell the property." Sobering words. The vote was taken
and the building program began with the contract being signed
that day. Architect Bert King told them that the building could be
used but not finished by June; the guest rooms would not be
ready, and the lounge might or might not be ready.

In quick action, nineteen days later, a ground-breaking ceremony was held on the "Rocking Chair Porch" of the old hotel building. *Kanuga News* reported in a special February 1967 edition: "It was a fitting tribute—the last gracious service that this old building rendered.... Today the ground on which she stood has been completely cleared.... The new complex will include a guest room wing, expanded dining room facilities, a lounge with panoramic views, classrooms, chapel, library, and a vastly expanded Rocking Chair Porch." There is a certain poetic irony that the same year in which the old Kanuga hotel was torn down, the old "Carolina Special" known to Kanugaites and Kanugans as the "Carolina Creeper" made its last run through Hendersonville on December 5, 1967. This was the best known of Southern Railway's passenger trains, making its first run from Charleston to Hendersonville en route to Cincinnati in January 1911, when Kanuga was a new and thriving private club. Kanugans was the name employed by George Stephens to describe the summer colony residents; Kanugaites was the name early used by the Episcopalians. The train had served both groups.

The new facility was completed, except for minor corrections and adjustments, and used as promised. At the Adult Conference, the Presiding Bishop and one of Kanuga's own, John E. Hines, was the keynoter. The two one-week social action conferences "were highlighted by the first Negro keynoters in Kanuga's history." The speakers were Leon Modeste of New York City, John Wheeler of Durham, and Vernon Jordan of Atlanta.

The official dedication was June 30, 1968. Some 350 attended the ceremonies. It had cost three-quarters of a million dollars. Bishop Henry presided at the event and board chairman Arrington made the main address. "We thank Almighty God that the old structure never burned; we were granted enough time without tragedy to do something different and better," he said. He also praised the architect, J. Bertram King, who he said "had captured the spirit of this blessed spot in a manner that is sheer genius." Ernest Patton, president of the new Kanuga Foundation, also spoke. Hartley was quoted in the Asheville newspaper stating, "The Inn now makes it possible for the first time for Kanuga to operate at least nine months out of the year. It will be available also, to those groups whose program is compatible with the philosophy of the Kanuga board, such as industry and other groups."

Summer 1968 at Kanuga was different for reasons other than facilities. Kanuga's new foundation was a fact. Hartley had initiated this reorganization which was approved at the December 1964 meeting of the Kanuga board. What had been a separate account that could be used as a revolving fund to meet cash shortages was now a separate Kanuga entity with its own board of directors. The foundation board had one representative from each of the owning dioceses and in 1968 held assets of $34,270.40. Hartley was executive director of the foundation.

John Arrington completed his second three-year term on Kanuga's board in 1968 and brought to a close his three-year tenure as board chairman. He liked to remind the board that one of the young counselors at an early Kanuga camp was a John E. Hines and one young man under his guidance at the camp was a Spartanburg boy named William C. Westmoreland. "Such a place is Kanuga to produce the leadership of the world," he proudly touted with the pride of one who first attended a Kanuga conference in 1928 and had not missed many years in between.

The development fund was in 1968 proceeding, if slowly. Some $240,859 had been received with pledges of $400,737 due in 1968 and $102,678 due within three years. Mortgage on the complex was $600,000. However, it was an up-beat board meeting that concluded the year. It was a year characterized by effective committee work and the creation of two committees—a Development Committee and a Promotion and Publicity Committee. Committees already in place were: Program, Property, and Finance. The Rev. L. Bartine Sherman was elected chairman of the board.

Committee chairmen with names new to Kanuga began reports and recommendations in the summer of 1969. At the summer Executive Committee meeting the following statement of purpose for restructuring was adopted:

> Our long-range goal, that of freeing Kanuga of financial dependence from both the owning dioceses and/or the local churches, should facilitate more sure progress and enable the board to guide Kanuga in reaching its full potential in serving the church and the world.

It was not a modest statement of goals. The very active program-planning committee chairman, Manney C. Reid of St. Stephens Church, Oak Ridge, Tennessee, had the assignment of putting into operation programs to that end. Fortunately, he was working from one of the most eclectic parishes in the church incorporating people from both science and industry. The committee planned and scheduled a weekend conference for late September dealing with the Special South Bend Convention, the second specially-called convention in the history of the church. The issue was The General Convention Special Program (GSCP), that is, funding to assist minority groups and other disadvantaged persons and how the money should or should not be spent. The reason for the Kanuga conference was "the feeling of the program group that many of our vestrymen and Church leaders are woefully ignorant in what is taking place within the larger Church."

The theme of the summer Adult Conference had been "The Church Listens to the World and Responds." Speakers were the Presiding Bishop's chairman for urban affairs, the president of the nation's largest Negro bank, a Peace Corps representative, and a representative from the Church and Industry Institute.[5] The Conference on Personal Religion featured a nationally recognized ecumenical faculty which included Lutheran and Roman Catholic clergy. The Family Conference brought resource people who had worked in the International Youth Exchange for the Episcopal Church, from the Japan Institute of Christian Education, and a physician specializing in psychoanalysis who had worked in both the church and the secular world. Bishop Pinckney received criticism from those asking the question of what happened to just the family vacation at Kanuga. Board chairman Sherman characterized Manney's work as "helping prepare for our constituency a framework in which they can better understand, and take their part in shaping, the rapid changes in church and society today."

At the close of the year, the board authorized the demolition of the old pavilion—long a fire hazard. Its replacement, however, would have to wait until the completion of the Development Campaign. Pledges at the end of the year totaled $430,000. The goal was not halfway there but the ambiguity that characterized the opening of the decade had been replaced by confidence in Kanuga's future both as to program and facilities. The new facilities fell considerably short of maximum utilization in the Young People's Conferences, but in most conferences and in the camps there was full utilization. The first year-round operation ended in the black and Kanuga was for most still the Kanuga of memories.

As the year 1969 ended, Edwin Voorhees of Morehead City, lay representative from the Diocese of East Carolina, was working as Kanuga's first lay board chairman. Philip Dietz had been added to the staff as operations superintendent, and executive director Ed Hartley was on the job for the long haul.

Chapter Eight
Internal Development

*The committee began to discern the continuing value of
the presence of this consultant.... His consultant services could also be retained to good advantage by the
Board of Directors, the Executive and other committees,
and by the Executive Director.* [1]

The Rev. Hunt Williams

The business management firm, Lee Associates, Inc., was
employed in 1960 to conduct a management engineering survey
of the organization and operation of Kanuga Conferences. The Lee
organizational review's purpose was to achieve a more effective
accomplishment of the objectives for which the organization was
formed. Hartley told the board in 1968 that, although the report
was laid away for several years and the recommendations not
seriously considered, he had leaned heavily on those recommendations the past few years.

When Philip Dietz from Reno, Nevada, by way of Cullman,
Alabama, was employed as operations superintendent, May 1,
1969, he was employed because he met the personal qualifica-
tions for the job and further the board had determined this to be
a job leading to operations manager. A consultant had helped
achieve this employment procedure. Only five years earlier John
Grainger had in effect written his own job description, "...my
understanding is that the job description and remuneration
details of my previous letter are acceptable to the board...." This
lack of a mutually-understood and mutually-accepted job description had had negative consequences. "The absence of clearly
defined policies in the areas of responsibility, authority, and

organization has resulted in working conditions most unpleasant," Bill Verduin had stated in his letter of resignation.

The Rev. William Jones, an Episcopal priest who directed the work of the Association for Christian Training and Service, an ecumenical consulting agency, had been employed by the board for consultative work. He had worked first with the Program Committee. One early task there was to put into context the type of programs Kanuga had been sponsoring as a necessary prelude to evaluating the programs. Kanuga programming fell into three areas: programs Kanuga planned, promoted, and carried out; programs Kanuga planned, promoted, but did not staff; and programs where Kanuga lent its facilities to other groups for their programming and staffing. Evaluation within this context enabled the committee to ascertain whether Kanuga programs were leading or following needs and interests of those who came to Kanuga.

Reid's committee concluded that "...our most positive area would have to be where we have rented out facilities. In the other two areas of programming we have not been too successful." A scheduled 1969 Kanuga-sponsored conference "Science for Clergy" had to be canceled for lack of interest. The 1970 successful "Impact of Science on Society" conference which brought distinguished public servants to Kanuga was not Kanuga sponsored. "This can only serve to point up the need for better efforts on the part of all those involved in Kanuga's programming." The Rev. Hunt Williams, a member of the Program Committee, working with the consultant William Jones, presented a comprehensive evaluation process in which every aspect of program planning and program execution would be reviewed. The board expressed its grateful appreciation for the profound contribution Manney Reid, from his Oak Ridge perspective, had made to Kanuga. He would serve on the committee for one year during the transition.

Reid also reminded the Executive Committee that a program building still was needed. It was not a question of simply needing more space. He said that the present complex used for program had not been intended or designed for this purpose. A program building was part of the original development program, he reiterated. He also suggested that the board look favorably at the idea of setting aside two consecutive weekends in October as Leaf Weekends with the week in between also available to fall guests.

In law it is called "an act of God," and carries special dispensations—the planned demolition of the pavilion was either a victim or beneficiary of just such an act. The 1970 ice storm caused considerable damage, and the insurance money was used to remove the fifty-nine-year-old building. This removal exposed a rare and beautiful view of the entire lake suggesting that the proposed new pavilion might better have a less obstructing position. The pavilion was included in the master plan and was projected to cost approximately $150,000.

Also in the spring of 1970, the long-planned new infirmary was becoming a reality. A grant of $10,000 to construct the building was made available to Kanuga from St. Peter's Hospital Foundation of Charlotte. Like most Kanuga buildings, it was set back in the woods. Paneled throughout, the building had a common room with a stone fireplace, an examination room, and four patient rooms. It was designed to be staffed during conference season with a nurse who had living quarters in the building.

Kanuga still had big mortgage payments. The fund-raising campaign seemed to have gone as far as it could go and needed to be revised. The capital funds campaign was yet to be completed and there was an agreement that again professional help would be necessary. William Whipple Associates of Lakeland, Florida, was selected. The firm was widely known in Episcopal church circles throughout the Southeast for conducting successful stewardship campaigns. The board agreed that the kick-off date would be January 15, 1971, and the stated goal was the liquidation of the mortgage on the present facility. The board approved the campaign "subject to the policies of the five owning dioceses and to such other areas as they present themselves." (The "other areas" were not defined.)

The Whipple Associates firm would provide a campaign director who would administer the entire campaign from Kanuga. Hartley would cooperate and participate in the whole operation. After six months, in June 1971, Whipple Associates reported that the campaign was below where it should be: on an over-all measurement, it was about 20 percent of what had been expected by that date.

There were 42 campaign areas. Thirteen had the planned kick-off meeting and eleven others did a bit to initiate a campaign. Whipple said that a sense of detachment pervaded the attitude of many people and many looked at Kanuga merely as a remote institution that had little if any connection with the life of the church.

Closer to Kanuga, in Asheville, one rector responded to Hartley's request for a lay person to help with the fund-raising by informing him that the diocesan conventions should have had an opportunity to respond and if the response was negative, then Kanuga should drop the whole idea. Besides he concluded: "We rather question that in general, people in the diocese would respond warmly to a fund-raising drive at Kanuga since we have just failed in this area of our response to National Church's need." This response fell under what Whipple Associates concluded was Kanuga's basic fund-raising problem—that it was perceived as competing with "local financial needs and accumulated problems of local parishes, and local drives for numerous purposes within the parish." Another immediate aspect of the campaign was that the executive employed by Whipple Associates to supervise the campaign resigned—leaving Hartley alone to carry on.

The Executive Committee concluded that Kanuga's contract with Whipple Associates should be concluded and that "no further payments would be made to the company until such time as the results of the campaign warrant the fulfillment of the contract as determined by the Executive Committee." The board the next day confirmed the recommendation and gave Hartley authority to continue the campaign and to determine its conclusion. In August 1971, the board and Whipple came to agreement on a settlement and in October the board budgeted $20,000 for the employment of a promotion person—male or female—and authorized $2,500 for a 16mm sound documentary to promote Kanuga.

The campaign had had some success. There were pledges in hand totaling $227,101 and Kanuga had learned a lot about itself. And while there had been dissatisfaction with some aspects of the way Whipple Associates had handled the Kanuga contract, it was an established and respected firm and its conclusion was worthy of consideration: "The 1971 Development Fund campaign has enlightened many of us, both as to Kanuga's special place in the Episcopal Church at large and the unique problems that are inherent in an institution with such diverse ownership and fiscal problems as envelope Kanuga."

Concurrent with the capital fund drive was the work of the Restructure Committee which the board had authorized to review the administrative structure of Kanuga. Bishop Pinckney had appointed this committee as one of his first acts after being elected board chairman in 1971. He appointed Bishop Fraser to serve as committee chairman. The other members were Gayle O. Averyt, board chairman and chief executive officer of Colonial Life & Accident Insurance Co., Columbia, South Carolina; William Morris, Jr., Asheville attorney; Louis M. Connor, Jr., vice-president, Development and Fund-Raising Consultants, Raleigh; and Edgar Hartley. The consultative services of William Jones were employed by the committee.

The committee met with accountants who specialized in hotel-motel operations and who had for many years served as auditors for Holiday Inns, and they also met with the holder of four Holiday Inn franchises for consultation and study, before beginning their report. While Kanuga could each year report that its accounts were in the black, that buildings from special designated gifts were adding to the increasingly magnificent property, and that attendance was increasing, there was a very dark side viewed from the perspective of professionals who knew hostelries, whatever their stated purposes. Kanuga was in debt to the Liberty Insurance Company of Greenville, South Carolina, for almost $600,000 and full support of the campaign drive for capital funds currently under way was necessary "if Kanuga is to survive its current financial crisis."

The study was completed in September and the general committee conclusion was: "The present board and owners are in the position of the farmer who found oil oozing through the soil of his land but did not have the time, equipment, or expertise to begin drilling." The Report of the Kanuga Study Committee was presented to the board first at its October meeting for initial review and then at the November meeting for action. In retrospect we can see that this committee again was saying that the recommendations drafted by Special Committee Appointed to Study Kanuga Conferences, 1964, could not be carried out under the current organizational structure.

Understandably the minutes in November 1971 record: "Considerable discussion took place regarding the proposed amended charter and bylaws and its effect on future operation of

Kanuga and centralizing responsibility and control through its Board of Directors." The proposed amended articles of incorporation and accompanying bylaws they were considering would, in fact, dissolve the 1950 Incorporation of Kanuga Conferences. A certificate of dissolution would be filed with the Secretary of State and then a new corporation would be formed. The structural changes that were being proposed would:

1. *Reduce the number and alter the manner of the selection of board members of no less than 15 or more than 20*

2. *Rewrite the bylaws so that members serve staggered terms of three years each and no more than two consecutive terms and that they be proposed by a nominating committee appointed by the executive committee*

3. *Provide each diocese to be represented by one bishop as an ex officio member of the board with voice and vote but not to be counted in determining a quorum*

4. *Provide directors to be selected on their ability to manage, develop, and promote Kanuga*

5. *Place the executive director in charge with staff employed and responsible to the directors*

6. *Adopt a system of reporting and bookkeeping such as used in hotels*

Kanuga would be organized much like a private church-related college with a self-perpetuating board.

Since the 1950 Kanuga Conferences, Inc., came into being the term "owning dioceses" had been descriptive of the legal ownership. The board was composed of diocesan bishops and members chosen by the conventions of the several dioceses. The plan under consideration would transfer the title of the land and buildings at Kanuga to the new corporation. There would be no "owning dioceses." In the unlikely event of the dissolution of the corporation—a determination the new corporation board alone (or a court order in case of bankruptcy) could make—the five dioceses would share in the disposition of any solvent assets.

The persuasive arguments which had been advanced for the reorganization were of such magnitude that all the bishops were able to support fully the proposed new corporate arrangement.

The meeting was at St. Peter's Church in Charlotte. Board member Beth Gash remembers it as a dark and dreary day. The meeting's purpose was for the old Board of Managers to vote themselves out of office. The legal work had been accomplished and the Articles of Amendment of Kanuga Conferences, Inc., were filed with the North Carolina Secretary of State the 20th day of January, 1972. Procedurally, the board was approving the new charter and bylaws and a new Board of Directors. They were being asked to select the new board from the names suggested by the Nominating Committee who had been selected for their experience in property management, investments, and hotel-motel-resort management. Those writing the history of Kanuga hereafter would not begin sentences with "The bishops..."

The first annual meeting of the new board in May 1972, at Kanuga, was obviously a different board meeting. Bishop Pinckney was the chairman. One new member was the Rev. Robert Parks of Trinity Parish, New York. Kanuga's new director of promotion, James L. Morton, was in attendance, just three weeks into his new job. Both executive director Edgar Hartley and operations superintendent Phil Dietz were there. Chief executive officer of Colonial Life & Accident Insurance, Gayle Averyt, board member from Columbia, presented some goals he felt could be realized over the next three years. These included "raising $200,000 over the next twelve months from the present fund-raising campaign; and working as rapidly as possible towards a full 60 percent utilization of Kanuga's facilities on a year-round basis, with a goal of a full ten percent increase each of the next three years." Averyt expected to do just that.

At the end of the summer season, the new director of promotion, J. L. Morton, reviewed with the Promotion and Publicity Committee the recommendations of the Harry Malone Associates evaluation of both the committee's work and the promotional directions the consulting firm was suggesting. The proposed parish contact of "Key Man" program should be changed to "Key Person" and the "Kanuga Conferences, Inc." as letterhead and advertising statement should give way to simply "Kanuga." The triangle in the logo should be constant in all advertising and the messages from Kanuga should be "up-beat." Further, Kanuga should advertise specific conferences and headliners in contrast to the past promotion of a summer package of conferences. From committee members came plans to update Kanuga mailing lists for the secular press. The Diocesan Press Service would regularly receive all Kanuga releases as would *The Episcopalian* and *The*

Living Church. The committee was advised that it should remember that Americans like to travel and that Kanuga should take advantage of this in order to fill Kanuga with those who simply liked to come to this beautiful place.

Serving on a Kanuga board became a time-consuming involvement. And it was, at times, frustrating. Publicity changes designed to enhance facility use such as separating the promotion of Camp Kanuga for Boys and Girls from the general conference schedule had been highly successful. "Camp registrations alone were running seventy percent ahead of last year at this time," was news readily applauded. But when the Kanuga Inn did not have breakfast for a couple who arrived one day early for a conference, their North Carolina medical doctor friend, who also was an old Kanuga friend, complained to the board, "Once before I have written to you about the situation at Kanuga which seems to me to be deteriorating into one of crass commercialism."

The May 1974 issue of the *Kanuga News* surprisingly was identified as Volume I, Number 1, with the explanation that since the old publication of the same name had become an occasional periodical, the new publication would be regular and it carried under the masthead the wording, "A Four Season Conference and Camping Center for Retreat, Renewal, and Inspiration." Internally, Kanuga was undergoing change. Bishop William J. Gordon, Jr., who had observed Kanuga in every stage of its development offered the observation that: "Church conferences and camps have been more a significant deepening factor in the spiritual life of the church than anything else the church has done." More specifically: "Kanuga is probably the most significant educational force in the church of the South and increasingly is becoming significant in the whole church." [2]

Writing about Kanuga becomes more difficult to organize and the format used in the literature of college and university writing becomes the obvious mode of presentation. Kanuga is an institution of higher education.

Conferences, Camps, and Retreats
1974–1983

Some 8,000 individuals came to Kanuga for conferences, camp sessions, special meetings, guest periods, or as client groups in 1974. The conference schedule was a Young People's

Conference, Christian Education Conference #1, followed a week later by Christian Education Conference #2, Adult Week #1, and Adult Week #2; then, a Guest Period in late July; and a period to enjoy October Leaves in the fall. Kanuga Camp for Boys and Girls had four sessions from early June through late August. The facilities were used intermittently throughout the year. The term "guest days"—one night's lodging plus three meals per person—was used to tally facility use and the 1974 number was in excess of 30,000. Some sixty-six not-for-profit church, governmental, and professional groups are included in the tally.

The camping sessions for boys and girls ages 8 to 15 were fun. Low-organized sports such as softball, volleyball, and basketball were an integral part of camp life. They were considered "pick-up and participate" activities and very little structure was needed on the part of the staff. The structural emphasis instead was spent in providing outdoor-living experiences. In a three-week session, each cabin camped out at least four times and sometimes as many as six or seven. Hikes to High Rock, Eagle Rock, and the Cow Pasture, along with cookouts, were camp highlights. Related to the outdoor-living experiences was the use of indigenous materials in the arts and crafts program. Vespers were daily and one 1974 camp session spent many busy hours rebuilding St. Andrew's Chapel at the north end of the lake.

The regular summer conference format was altered in 1975 to include a music conference and a conference on spiritual renewal in the church. In late August 1975, Kanuga sponsored a two-day Charismatic Conference. The reason given was the "Program Committee's concern that Kanuga impact the charismatic movement with theology and teaching more in keeping with our Anglican and catholic heritage than charismatic Episcopalians are otherwise likely to encounter elsewhere." The committee expressed its intentions to continue this interest in the movement.

Ed Hartley once described the Program Committee as "the lifeblood of Kanuga." The Rev. Dudley E. Colhoun, Jr., of Winston-Salem, began initiating some conference schedule changes during the four years, 1970–1974, when he was program chairman. It was during his tenure as chairman of the committee that Kanuga moved from a summer-only to a year-round operation. He was followed in that job in 1975 by the Rev. James Fenhagen, director of the church and ministry program of the ecumenical Hartford Seminary Foundation. There he worked with congregations and conducted research on the church and society. He had been involved with Kanuga for over twenty years when he accepted the assignment. There were eight Kanuga-sponsored conferences in 1976.

Kanuga program publicity was designed to pique interest and bring those interested in a particular subject or topic to Kanuga. They came for study and fellowship with others who shared the same concerns. Kanuga provided a leader. The leader was selected because of recognized experience. A review of Kanuga Program Committee minutes suggests real effort at getting the best informed leaders possible. There was no suggestion of a restriction on the speaker's presentation or theological perspective. The conference was not a seminar, or class, or workshop, and yet it was all of these. It was intellectual and it was not doctrinaire and it was this characteristic perhaps that most set Kanuga apart from other religious conference centers. "It belongs to the Anglican way to put a high premium on the mind. Unless the mind is satisfied, the heart's emotions will not sustain us long," the Archbishop of Canterbury George Carey said at St. James' Church, Hendersonville, 1993, while at a Kanuga meeting. This describes the Kanuga conferences from the very first.

"Where do we go from here?" This was the discussion topic of a 1976 Program Committee meeting at Kanuga. During the summer, some 1,500 people attended Kanuga conferences. "There is a market for the people," the committee reasoned. Their research had found a lot of interest in the vestry retreat idea but no interest in conferences for women only. "Some thoughts on futuristic thinking are expressed. What are the trends today? ...retirement at 55; homosexuality; divorce and remarriage...What kinds of institutional response to these trends should be considered?"

The Program Committee announced early in 1977 that there were 22 Kanuga conferences scheduled for that summer—200 percent more than the previous year. This was a major change in the pattern that had been followed so long with only minor modifications. This Chautauqua of conferences addressed personal problems; living and growing with the years; the Bible for living; travels in the faith; spiritual growth; and marriage enrichment. Special conferences for the clergy were: increasing job mobility; management in the local parish; interim ministers; and renewal of the Holy Spirit in the parish. There was a House of Bishops seminar on placement; implications of the Book of Common Prayer changes; and evangelism wherever. Dying, described as life's final stage of growth, was also a conference theme.

The Board of Directors in 1978 was told in a report from its Long-Range Planning Committee: "Kanuga should continue to broaden its programs in ways which can better meet the needs of parishes over a wider range than the Carolinas. As the keystone of this effort, we recommend that Kanuga establish an Institute of Parish Life, under a full-time program director, and the major thrust of that program, year-round, should be support of clear and established parish needs throughout the Province." It identified those needs as Christian education, music and liturgy, stewardship, vestry training, and theological support.

"When someone asks me what to expect at Young People's Conference, I tell them 'Try not to have any expectations.' Each week is different. You have to be prepared for just about anything. Just be open-minded." Margaret Blank had seen the Young People's Conference grow from 78 people in five states in 1976 to 204 participants from 11 states in 1981. She came to Kanuga first at age 13 and kept a scrapbook which recorded her Kanuga days and as a college freshman shared those memories with the *Kanuga News.* "For me, Kanuga '76 had been a beginning of one phase of my life and '81 the end of that phase and the beginning of another," was another diary entry she shared.

In January 1980, Kanuga and the Episcopal Foundation for Drama began a pilot program offering training in speech and drama. Doris Dargan, a leader of community church drama in Spartanburg and one who had conducted drama at Kanuga for over twenty-five years, directed the program. Anthony Ridley who had toured with the New York-based National Shakespeare Company was the resident drama director the first summer. Viewed as an experiment and financed by Spartanburg's Advent church members plus Mrs. Dargan, the program brought drama back to Kanuga. Mummy and Scotty Robertson had put on Gilbert and Sullivan plays back in 1937. Ridley's work, however, was serious drama. With Liza Howe of Hendersonville, they presented "Love's Labours," a Shakespearean love scene pastiche. With summer staff member Frank Creamer joining them, they collaborated in a Wolf Mankowitz comic play about Jonah's attempt to escape from God. On the waterfront, a summer group did "Noah's Flood" and in the Chapel of the Transfiguration, a modern moralist play, "Arks, Bridges, and Rainbows," was performed twice.

Beginning in January 1981, Kanuga began a theologian-in-residence program. The program would provide for the serious theology student, lay or clergy, a resource person of recognized academic standing; and a theologian would bring more theological perspective to Kanuga program development. The Very Rev. Urban T. Holmes, dean of the School of Theology, The University of the South, did the five-month trial run and concluded:

> *Enough has been accomplished to make it imperative that this program go on. We began by taking some of the things that were happening, such as vestry weekends and the six Parish Family Weekends, and offered a theological component to them. We also designed some new programs: the week-long conference Spiritual Pathways for Mature Christians, a lay-invitational seminar, and a four-day conference on Being a Priest Today.*

Further, he wrote that he had hopes "for the future of Kanuga as a place for serious theological reflection."

Both the drama program and the theologian-in-residence were pilot programs. After two summers at Kanuga, Anthony Ridley began working with a Shakespearian company at the College of William and Mary, and Mary Nicholson, also of Spartanburg, accepted direction of the Kanuga drama and continued the work in conjunction with the Episcopal Foundation for Drama. It was only natural then for "Spring Fest—82" to host the Coventry Cathedral Choir and Liturgical Dancers in a three-day conference in April when Kanuga was in bloom.

The death of "Terry" Holmes in August 1981, just after he had returned from study in England and Scotland, precluded his helping the Program Committee advance the program he had begun. The committee continued to pursue the idea in a possible academy of theology and Christian ministry for laity and clergy. The possibility of serious discourse that included laity, clergy, and a theologian is not common in the church.

Kanuga News in April 1982 reported the death of Laura

Smith Ebaugh in her home community, Greenville, South Carolina. She was a retired Furman University professor. She had a
summer home near Kanuga and was said never to have missed an
Adult Conference. During this time she heard the great speakers
and writers of her church in the informal setting that was a
Kanuga conference. Those who were here frequently, like Bishop
FitzSimons Allison, she knew. She even knew his mother who was
involved in early Kanuga days. Ebaugh had been the physical
director of girls at Camp Capers in 1921, one of the Kanuga
forerunners. She wrote a chapter about these early times in the
book her friend Catherine "Bee" Finlay edited, *Early Kanuga
Memories.* Ebaugh wrote: "I taught a course in 'Faith and Conduct' for the teenage girls. When I asked the bishop (Finlay) what
I should include, he replied, 'Just let them talk and help them
think out their problems.' I tried to do this." Whether it be in her
assignment or in 1982 Scott Peck's discussion of his nationally-
recognized book, *The Road Less Traveled,* the Kanuga purpose
had been constant.

Finance and Promotion
1974–1983

"Kanuga required $200,000 a year over and above operating
income not only to meet principal and interest payments, but also
to provide essential maintenance and to support capital expendi-
tures," George Esser, chairman of the Long-Range Planning
Committee told the second annual weekend meeting of the
Kanuga Board of Visitors when they met in October 1979.
Executive director Edgar Hartley told the visitors: "Kanuga is now
moving from its struggle for survival into a new struggle for real
financial stability."

The creation of the Board of Visitors was part of the board's
strategy to achieve this financial stability. Also with a board
chosen for reasons other than diocesan representation, it was
important to reestablish diocesan links. Vox populi is vital. Board
minutes are obscure about the origin of the Board of Visitors. A
note to Albert Gooch at the time of the 1993 death of Kirk Finlay
is the first written account of its origin. Robert Haden wrote to
Gooch: "There's one thing that needs to be known if you don't
know it. Kirk was the driving force behind the Board of Visitors.
He came up with the idea originally. He pushed for it for several

years before it got started." (Kirkman Finlay, Jr., was the grandson of Bishop Finlay.)

In the fall of 1974, Matt Mattison and Clifford Shirley had outlined for the newly-reorganized Board of Directors' Executive Committee a plan to raise over the next five years $700,000 to pay off all indebtedness. The plan also would put in place a new sewage disposal plant that recent state legislation mandated, acquire two tracts of land now surrounded by Kanuga property and needed for Kanuga's road development, and either replace the old cottages or add a new wing to the Inn. They would also develop a capital reserve that would preclude borrowing and interest payments on needed capital. Gayle Averyt restated the Kanuga conundrum for the Executive Committee: "It appears Kanuga needs annually $100,000 raised from outside sources to carry the additional financing necessary for mortgage loan and interest."

"Kanuga—Its Place in Your Life" was an attractive booklet that introduced the 1974 Annual Giving Program and inaugurated the Kanuga Investors Club. These were to be annual gifts of $250; $500; $1,000; $3,000; $5,000; and onetime $25,000 gifts with titles to designate the level of giving. Donors would be honored by having their names on a published list each year. This was a college and university fund-raising technique that had been successfully employed by those institutions for many years. Mrs. A. B. Stoney of Morganton, North Carolina, gave the first lifetime gift which served as the cornerstone of the campaign.

Also there was need to reach out to Kanuga devotees for financial support in amounts that would vary according to their ability to contribute. In place was a Memorial Fund, a way to make a memorial contribution with the donor's name inscribed in a memorial book that was kept in the Chapel. The board decided to give this more visibility by publishing each December all memorials given during the year although not the amount. In 1975, a John A. Pinckney Scholarship Fund was set up by the board to honor Bishop Pinckney who had been part of the establishment of Kanuga. The Fund would assist those who wanted to come to Kanuga but were unable to afford the entire fee.

The Kanuga Episcopal Program Fund campaign got under way in October 1976, with Episcopalians in Winston-Salem pledging $60,000 in Phase I of the drive which intended in time to raise $300,000. Over $100,000 was needed immediately to upgrade the waste treatment plant and to permit liquidation of loans to free funds for more programming. The campaign would begin in Charleston, Charlotte, and Columbia, the areas of especially strong Kanuga support. These were named "bellwether areas" and were targeted for Phase I giving. The designation was to suggest that other areas follow the sheep which leads the flock with its bell ringing. Phase II would encompass all areas of the two Carolinas which enjoyed Kanuga's facilities.

At the same time, but not a part of this formal drive, St. Paul's Church, Winston-Salem, North Carolina, made a gift of $100,000 to be used toward the construction of the long-talked-about and hoped-for new recreation building. The gift was from that church's Legacy Fund. The building was already in the planning stages and would include a gym for basketball and volleyball and in general fill the need for an indoor recreation center. Kanuga had been without indoor recreational space since the pavilion was torn down in 1970. The generous gift was $75,000 short of the amount needed to build. A special development committee was set up to raise this money and board member John D. Clark accepted the assignment to raise the money and raise it apart from the major drive under way at the same time. A second gift from the Winston-Salem church's Legacy Fund plus a gift from Spartan Food Systems of Spartanburg (currently, Flagstar Companies, Inc.) rounded out the needed funding. The building was dedicated in 1978 as part of the first meeting of the newly-formed Board of Visitors. Interestingly, it was at the second meeting of the Board of Visitors in 1979 that vestry members of St. Paul's, Winston-Salem, became aware of the need to winterize the building and then soon gave an additional $35,000 for that purpose. Again, the gift was from the parish Legacy Fund, a fund endowed primarily by bequest of Serena and Wilson Dalton.

The Episcopal Program Fund Drive had no formal conclusion. In this it was like the drives which had gone before it. The immediate crisis was past. The drive had, however, given publicity to real problems that took money to solve. The Diocese of Western North Carolina's foundation gave $15,000 for a sewage disposal plant. In 1977 about one-half of all who attended Kanuga conferences were here for the first time. Their response typically was more than positive and also each was a new recruit to the Kanuga "boosters club," which in promotion terms means each now was on the mailing list. "We just keep treading successfully, with real effort," Gayle Averyt told the board one more time in October 1977. "The justification for this debt is the fact that Kanuga's dollar assets and its liquidation value far exceed the debts."

Gayle Averyt's term both as board member and Finance Committee chairman ended in 1980. This pending departure led the Executive Committee to review Kanuga's organization, especially the role of the executive director and the structure of the Board of Directors. Averyt's commitment of time was beyond what reasonably could be expected of one accepting this committee assignment. It was the thrust of the discussion. How Kanuga's management structure should be defined relative to the committee chairs and just what was the job of a board member were discussed.

Ray F. West, who had been appointed director of administration in 1977, in January 1982 reported that the previous financial year was outstanding. From an operational standpoint, he told them, July and August were the two most profitable months financially in Kanuga's history. In April 1982, West presented the long-awaited news: the March mortgage payment on the Inn had been made on time and remaining were two $30,612 payments, due in September and again in March 1983. He carried the last payment to the bank in person. *Kanuga News* reported the glad tidings. "It is clear that the overall picture for Kanuga as of this date is a little ahead of 1981 and it appears to be an excellent year developing both during the summer, the spring, and fall," Hartley echoed the tidings to the Executive Committee.

The Board of Directors in March 1982 reviewed their "Wish List" of Kanuga's continuing needs. Such basic needs as private baths in the Inn, that is, converting the existing connecting bathrooms into two private baths, were high items on the list. The list also included scholarship aid because Kanuga was expensive especially when the cost of travel must be included in the budget to attend a Kanuga conference. The economy was good and board member John Flanagan commented, "If we recognize the need for such a program, then we should get on with it." Kanuga would plan for a two-million-dollar capital campaign to begin in April of 1983. Ed Hartley had announced to the board that he planned to retire in 1983 and several on the board thought it wise to hold the campaign while he was still at Kanuga and the drive could take advantage of his twenty years of experience. The vote for the drive was unanimous.

Buildings and Grounds
1974–1983

In May 1974, work on the program building—the Balthis Building—was under way. In 1971, Kanuga had received a gift of $75,000, payable over the following six years, from the Pearl Dixon Balthis Foundation to finance a program building which would be named in honor of William Leonard Balthis and Pearl Dixon Balthis. The architect chosen was J. Bertram King, the same architect who had designed Kanuga Inn. The building would be 78.8 x 76.8 feet with a 60 x 62 foot auditorium. It would be able to seat between 250 and 300 depending on the arrangement for the particular event. Side doors that could be opened in the summer converted the building into an open-air facility ideal to accommodate larger summer numbers. Completed in September, the building served in some way every group that came to Kanuga since its completion as an auditorium, place for seminars, round-table discussions, square dances—all evidence of the need for such a program building. In no time walkways were lighted, the grounds landscaped, and rock walls of native stone gave it a feeling of belonging. Suffragan bishop of the Diocese of North Carolina and board president W. Moultrie Moore presided at the dedication November 9, 1974.

Also in May 1974, another building by another architect was in progress. Architect Luther Lashmit of Winston-Salem had prepared plans to remodel and expand the Children's Activity Center. The work was done by the Kanuga maintenance department. The old 70 x 20 foot Baker Hall was renovated and the rooms enlarged and pine paneled and made more suitable for big activities that involve lots of little children. The framed Disney pictures on the walls were a gift from Disney World. One is an original transparency from the "Bambi" movie.

Also in May 1974, work begun by the Kanuga maintenance department back in March was completed and under the breeze-way between the Inn and sleeping accommodations were three new classrooms. The rooms measured 16 x 16 feet and were comfortable for groups up to about 20 with large windows over-looking the lake on one side and the Inn's courtyard on the other.

Also beginning in May 1974, Phil Dietz kept *Kanuga News* readers informed of what was happening to the buildings and on the grounds of Kanuga. A column "From Phil" let the readers know what was happening in their absence. Actually, it was chock full of information that the Kanugaite and one who would tell the Kanuga story in years to come would like to know. For instance, twenty trees were being planted for each one that was cut either to accommodate building or because of the age of the relatively short-lived pines.

Kanuga in 1974 also hosted the Arrington family members for the dedication of Saint John's Chapel. The Chapel, downstairs in the dining wing, was and is a much-used space that was made functional by a gift in honor of John White Arrington III. The bishop of South Carolina, Gray Temple, presided at the July 17th dedication.

The old camp site (west camp) was modernized in 1974 to attract youth groups and did attract the North Carolina Choir Camp, High School Band Camp, Girl Scouts, and the National Wildlife Association (as the organization was named at that time). This was service Kanuga could offer compatible with its stated purposes and it was an income-producing mechanism which Kanuga had relied on since its earliest days. Possibly $30,000 could help offset the inflation that was so hurting Kanuga at this time, Hartley reasoned. The National Wildlife Federation, which is the country's largest private, nonprofit conservation organization, in 1974 leased the Kanuga facilities as a site for its Wildlife Camp. There were two 12-day sessions that summer for boys and girls 11 to 14 years of age. The program has remained at Kanuga ever since.

Today there are ten rustic cabins, each accommodating 14 campers and two staff members. College students from all over the United States are recruited as staff. The National Wildlife Federation's 1993 information for campers describes Kanuga: "It is an extremely lush area offering a good variety of hardwoods, shrubs, grasses, and wildflowers. Included in your programming planning packet will be basic species lists for birds, amphibians, reptiles, mammals, trees, plants, ferns, and shrubs of the area."

A forest management plan developed by Merrill-Wilson forest consultants of Hendersonville was put in place in 1977. Kanuga white pines were over-mature and in need of harvest while some profit could be extracted from the cutting. Unattended growth results in dead trees which must be removed as unusable wood. Proper growth and proper cutting result both in profitable tree cutting and with wildlife, water quality, and erosion control all enhanced. The cuttings at that time garnered some $40,000 and the reforestation program that would continue was begun with that cutting. Without question, the presence of the National Wildlife Federation over the years has had a profound influence on the environmental and conservation awareness at Kanuga.

A major property committee project was announced in the spring of 1979. A cluster of possibly five or six new cottages would be built as soon as practical. They were called "cottages" in keeping with the Kanuga custom; they were, in fact, year-round guest houses and they were the first cottages constructed at Kanuga in seventy years. This was one of the most active phases of Kanuga development. The result was that more people and parishes could come to Kanuga for programs at any time of the year. The donors of the cottages would have special priority in reserving the cottages. The cottages would be compatible to Kanuga cottage style, be on a hillside and convenient to the Inn, and would have vehicle access. The first cottage was named Grace Church Cottage. It was a gift of Mr. and Mrs. Nolan Galloway of Ocala, Florida. It was dedicated at the annual meeting of the Board of Visitors, October 1979.

The cottage idea quickly captured the interest of several families with a Kanuga tradition. The second cottage was begun in the fall of 1979, a gift from the Pritchard family of Charleston, South Carolina. It was given in honor of Edward and Julia Pritchard. Like Grace Church Cottage, the Pritchard cottage had four bedrooms, two baths, and porches. Both have fireplaces. St. John's Cottage followed in 1981. The cottage was given by Richard D. Austin and Judy B. Austin, communicants of St. John's Church, Charlotte, North Carolina, in memory of their parents.

When the Board of Visitors met in October 1982, their fifth gathering, they shared in the dedication of the Austin cottage and saw the cleared ground where the fourth cottage would be built. This cottage was a second cottage gift of the Pritchard family and was, in time, designated as a memorial to Edgar Hartley. A fifth cottage would honor Kanuga board member Ben S. Willis, the Visitors were told at the meeting. It was made possible by Mrs. Willis, her children, and St. Paul's Church, Winston-Salem.

The five new cottages—now called Guest Houses—increased the October through April capacity by 40, allowing 180 guests in what used to be Kanuga's "off season."

One interesting and hard-to-get-to shelter on top of Wolf Mountain overlooking the French Broad River valley and the city of Hendersonville provides the hiker a bit of shelter from the rain but also is a monument to the diversity of Kanuga Conferences. Late in August 1980, Camp Kanuga was used by a group of 57 persons from 11 states for the first intentional living program held at Kanuga. The week was devoted to simple, thoughtful living, work, play, worship, and reflection. Simple foods prepared in a community kitchen reflected the world's need for a responsible diet. The shelter the group jointly built stands near the spot where Rufus Morgan used to take groups of silent hikers to watch the sun rise.

Maintenance at Kanuga was performed at this time by four men. Together they had worked at Kanuga for a collective total of nearly 100 years according to the calculations of Phil Dietz. Reggie Revis who retired in 1974 started working for Kanuga shortly after the church acquired it. Roy Guice, George Guice, and Coy Johnson all were raised in the immediate neighborhood. Roy and George had worked at Kanuga at times before World War II and then after the war returned to North Carolina and in time came back to Kanuga. Coy returned to Kanuga after completing 20 years of military service. Dietz and his staff also both designed and built the new maintenance building using wood cut on the property. The large building is on a hillside next to the west camp facility and houses indoor storage areas plus a shop.

Kanuga in the early 1980s received a grant from the Diocese of Upper South Carolina for a study of retirement and its relationship to Kanuga. The grant was augmented by a grant from the Diocese of East Carolina. Should Bishop Finlay's idea of a Kanuga with family-owned dwelling houses—and it would be retirement housing principally—be revived? John V. Flanagan, board member and a retired DuPont manager, headed the investigation which contracted Barbara Baker Freiman Associates of Lenoir, North Carolina, consultant in retirement housing, to conduct a feasibility study of such housing. Of the 368 responses received, 60 percent expressed interest in moving to a retirement community at Kanuga. The Hendersonville area was already a major retirement center and the idea of a private reserve seemed appealing to many who had loved Kanuga. With this information in hand, the board in October 1982 authorized their consultant to begin the next phase of the study, a presentation of a suggested overall construction plan and pro forma estimates of development costs.

Personnel
1974–1983

When the Board of Visitors gathered at Kanuga in October 1980, board member George Esser told them—some 111 members—in a presentation on long-range planning: "We are trying to expand Kanuga without losing the values that make it so meaningful to so many people." Growth mandates the employment of additional personnel. The challenge then becomes personnel selection and job definition. When Bill Verduin took the Kanuga executive director's job his wife was employed as his secretary and together they administered Kanuga. In 1974, there were an office manager and a program director along with a secretarial staff to do the paper work required to administer a $400,000 cash-flow institution that rapidly was becoming a twelve-month operation.

James Morton resigned as director of promotion in October 1973. Hartley had identified the job as broad in scope and Morton expressed his frustration in his last report to the program committee when he told them that it always was his understanding that "his effort was to be two-fold, communication/public relations and sales, which meant filling current programs to 100 percent utilization and off-season use to 60 percent utilization." With Kanuga's growth, employee performance expectancy and what a person reasonably could be expected to do were in need of redefinition.

Monroe M. Ashley, a Baptist minister, was appointed promotion director January 1, 1974. Prior to the Kanuga job, Ashley was for five years director of Camp Ridgecrest Camp for Boys, earlier a chaplain at the University of North Carolina-Greensboro, and at one time, a management consultant for the Baptist Sunday School Board in Nashville. A short regularly-scheduled column in *Kanuga News* permitted him to introduce himself to the Episcopal readers. He resigned in October 1975 to become executive director of the Presbyterian conference center at Montreat.

Frank C. Ballard, Jr., was appointed director of promotion in October 1976. Previously employed as advertising and publicity writer for Price/McNabb Advertising Agency, Asheville, he also had been a newspaper reporter for the *Lexington Dispatch.* He immediately began Kanuga promotional advertising in both *The Episcopalian* and *The Christian Century.* He told the board that advertising in 1981 had produced a dollar return of 2-to-1 for the expenditure. Ballard was interested in Kanuga's history and in 1978 put together a useful summary of Kanuga's first fifty years.

Ballard identified the annual program brochure as the single most important element in Kanuga's promotion. He developed it from a poster-sized "crowded" fold sheet to a 16-page program catalogue and maintained a mailing list in excess of 8,000. He advertised Kanuga at the national convention of the church and developed a relationship with the board which minutes often characterized with approval.

George A. Oldham was appointed director of administration in March 1976, and was followed in early 1977 by Ray West who prior to the Kanuga appointment had been general manager of Scottish Inn in Gastonia. An Asheville native, Episcopalian, and University of North Carolina graduate in economics, Ray had also studied philosophy at Oxford University and had served as a navy lieutenant. Hartley had told the Board of Directors in November 1975 that he needed a person in internal affairs so he could spend more time with the board and with the many sub-committees. At this time, Hartley acted as secretary to many of the board sub-committees. There were many meetings. About 45 persons were participating in program planning with carefully prepared reports following each meeting. Also Hartley was having some health problems, although he reported to the board in November that he "now had a clean bill of health from his doctors."

The Rev. LaRue Downing was named director of programs in May 1980. He had for six years previous to his appointment worked as a senior trainer in human relations for the Mid-Atlantic Training Committee and prior to that was rector of St. John's Church, Wilmington. He had in 1978 served on the staff of Kanuga's Spirituality Conference. He was a Virginia Theological Seminary graduate.

Camp director Don Jones who had directed Camp Kanuga since 1975 resigned in 1982 and was replaced by Jerry Courtney.

Jerry had been on the staff for the previous six years as assistant director and had prepared Camp Kanuga for accreditation by the American Camping Association. Prior to coming to Kanuga he had been youth director of Rock Chapel United Methodist Church in Atlanta. He held a bachelor's degree from Berry College and had studied recreational administration at the University of Georgia.

Carol Black joined the Kanuga staff in the fall of 1977 as reservation manager, assigning rooms and allocating the meeting space, which in 1977 was most limited. Because she recognized that the initial guest contact is the room reservation, Carol established a rule for the Kanuga hostelry that the pressures of the reservation office or at the desk should never be apparent to the guests. Learning quickly who wanted what cottage or what room and understanding the reasons for such requested accommodations, Carol established a rapport with guests which has become legend.

The relationship between staff personnel and the chief executive officer of a board and the committees of the board are more perplexing in a volunteer organization than in the business world. Hartley, in a 1981 memorandum to the board, attempted to summarize these complexities as he anticipated his announced 1983 retirement. The board committees work with staff personnel in getting the information necessary to fulfill their responsibilities. Accordingly, the board respects the counsel of staff personnel in its deliberations. How that relationship then relates back to the staff personnel's dealings with the board has special implications for the board's chief executive officer and at Kanuga was never resolved to Hartley's satisfaction.

The Rev. Dudley Colhoun, Jr., rector of St. Paul's Church, Winston-Salem, North Carolina, was elected president of the Kanuga board of directors in 1979. He was followed in 1980 by the Rt. Rev. Thomas A. Fraser of the Diocese of North Carolina. Bishop Fraser long had been involved in Kanuga's development, including the restructuring of the organization in the early 1970s. Colhoun also had a long Kanuga record of involvement. Both were aware of unresolved personnel problems that needed serious attention.

Early in 1982, at the request of the board, George Esser reviewed Kanuga's management situation and concluded that while no expensive management study was required, the basic structure of Kanuga and the role of the board, the executive director, and the committees should be reviewed. An appropriate time to change by-laws would be at the time a new executive director came aboard. He would have a proposal for the October meeting.

Edgar Hartley, Jr., died May 13, 1982, at his home in Hendersonville. He was sixty-four years old. Bishop Hunley Elebash prepared a statement expressing the sentiment of the board:

> *His leadership became primary in Kanuga's life and epito-*
> *mized those qualities which called all of us to our best personal*
> *achievement. His hopes and dreams for Kanuga were always*
> *lofty, and thereby Kanuga's pilgrimage and journey aimed*
> *toward service to God's Church and Family. His devotion and*
> *the devotion of his wife, Mary, are noted on this day by*
> *Kanuga's Board of Directors in gratitude and affection and*
> *love.*

October 15, 1982

∂Ⅎ𝒮

Chapter Nine
Toward National Service

In the peaceful setting of Kanuga Episcopal Conference Center in North Carolina, USA, we have experienced fellowship together.... This is probably the nearest I'll get to God here on Earth. [1]

The Most Rev. George Carey, Archbishop of Canterbury

Kanuga was not ready to replace Ed Hartley. He had secured for himself a place in the history of the institution that would be difficult to fill. Bishop Finlay before him had earned this honor. However, scheduled conferences were continuing at Kanuga even as his funeral rites were being conducted. The executive committee asked John V. Flanagan to accept administrative leadership until a search committee could be appointed and new leadership found. Dr. Flanagan lived in nearby Flat Rock and, as a board member since 1980, was knowledgeable about the job he was undertaking. He was sixty-five years old and a chemist, who while employed with DuPont had worked on the Manhattan Project. A search committee was immediately set in motion.

During the eleven months Dr. Flanagan was acting director of Kanuga, he did not consider his assignment as interim caretaker. Executive secretary and office manager Ann McKinney has observed, "Dr. Flanagan made possible some employee benefits which had only been a dream before. Kanuga has moved forward at a tremendous pace during and since the tenure of John Flanagan."

At the October 1982 meeting of the Board of Directors, the by-law revisions George Esser and Charles Shaffer had been instructed to work on were introduced to the board and were accepted. The changes would structure the board along the same lines corporations had found to be effective. The significant changes included:

—*Kanuga's chief operating officer who has in the past been known as the executive director now will be known as the president of the corporation. The president is made a voting member of the board.*

—*The chief executive officer who has in the past been called the president of the board will now be called the chairman of the board. Similarly, the vice-president of the board becomes the vice-chairman.*

—*The board is increased in number from 25 to 27, and will include the president.*

—*The executive committee was authorized to conduct business between meetings of the board.*

Albert S. Gooch, Jr., at a called meeting of the Kanuga board in Charlotte, December 11, 1982, was named president of Kanuga. He would be on the job April 1, after completing his obligations as director of admissions at The University of the South, Sewanee, Tennessee. This would put him on the job in time to begin the busy summer conference schedule. Gooch had been director of admissions at the university since 1970 and worked in the school's development office as executive director of the Associated Alumni from 1965-70. He was 44 years old and had taught English and history at Sewanee Military Academy from 1960 to 1964. He was married to Carol Jean (Jeannie) Arrington and had one son, Albert Sidney (Tres), and a daughter, Alyson. Both Gooch and his wife were from Mississippi. Gooch was an active layman in the Diocese of Tennessee, serving as layreader, vestryman, and sometime warden at churches in and around Sewanee.

President Gooch's first Kanuga board meeting was April 22, 1983, twenty-two days into the job. Board chairman Bishop William A. Beckham asked Gooch to discuss his first three weeks on the job. He said that he anticipated that the proposed capital funds campaign would be challenging and exciting, but defining Kanuga's purpose and direction should come first. A number of areas needed attention, he observed: the old cottages, operations and personnel policies, and the vacant director of program position. LaRue Downing had in November resigned the Kanuga job to become rector of the Church of the Good Shepherd in Augusta, Georgia. The often-discussed "life estates policy," retirement community possibilities, re-routing the entry road, and the need for strengthening ties with the Episcopal Church were also on the list of concerns he wanted to investigate. He said he would have proposals for the board to consider in the fall.

The Capital Funds Drive

The successful capital funds drive set the pace for Kanuga for the decade and accordingly becomes the preface to understanding those years. Encouraged by the fact that Kanuga was out of debt for the first time since 1966, the board voted in its fall meeting, October 11-12, 1984, to proceed with the campaign. The goal would be $1.5 million. The stated purpose was not to make Kanuga bigger—or to change its nature. Rather: "Improvements were needed to make Kanuga safer, more comfortable, and better equipped to serve its constituents' needs, and to make it financially secure," President Gooch said to the board. Anticipating all that is involved in a capital funds drive Gooch cautioned, "Let us remember that, as said in the marriage service, this is 'not to be entered into unadvisedly or lightly, but deliberately.'"

Included among the major needs and goals were:

—*$250,000*   *to build a bypass to eliminate the dangerous situation of having a state highway running through the center of Kanuga*

—*$250,000*   *cottage renovations*

—*$250,000*   *to purchase what was called the Fuller-Drake property to guard against encroachment in a rapidly growing county*

—*$150,000*   *for the Edgar Hartley, Jr. Program Enrichment Endowment*

—*$ 80,000*   *to build a program building in the new cottage area*

—*$ 20,000*   *to improve Kanuga's water system*

—*$500,000*   *assorted needs*

Ketchem, Inc., North Carolina, was employed for fund-raising counsel and Edward K. Pritchard, Jr., was asked to be general chairman of the campaign. The budget for campaigning was $40,000, which was modest by almost any fund-raising standard. The campaign proposed focusing on individuals with the greatest giving potential. This would not be a wide approach across the several dioceses, the way past Kanuga campaigns had been conducted. Rather, the Kanuga leadership would be the first asked to give—the Board of Directors, the Board of Visitors, and finally the staff. The second group asked to give would be some 100 prospects with the potential of $25,000 or greater. Then 250 to 300 people with prospects from $5,000 to $24,999 would be asked. Finally those who would be identified for special gifts with the expectancy of $5,000 or less would be contacted.

At the onset it was recognized that the campaign's success would be dependent upon several factors. First was careful planning and research. The commitment of the staff and the Board of Directors to give personally and to make calls on behalf of the campaign was essential. Finally, those persons not on the board but who had long-time personal and even longer family ties to Kanuga must be visited and personally enlisted in the campaign. If all these groups gave and gave generously, then the chances of success were good. The board realized that it faced a crucial test, one which would determine the future of Kanuga.

And they did it! The goal for the Kanuga staff, the Board of Directors, and Board of Visitors, was $900,000 and those three groups surpassed the mark in mid-January. The Capital Funds Campaign deadline for conclusion was June 15, 1985. A surprise gift arrived in July to push the campaign total over $1.6 million. Counting the money given to renovate cottages before the campaign began (which would have been added to the campaign goal had it not already been promised), the total given and pledged for capital purposes over the past two years was almost two million dollars. This was the first Kanuga drive ever to have a formal conclusion when there could be a celebration of a goal achieved.

Buildings and Grounds
1983–1993

In the president's report to the Board of Directors in October 1985, now that the campaign for capital funds had come to such a happy ending, was the announcement: "And so we begin to use the campaign income."

The first priority was the road bypass. The old road, a state highway, ran directly through Kanuga's greatest concentration of buildings and therefore had the greatest amount of foot traffic. Kanuga was powerless to control the speed or volume of vehicular traffic. The procedure to get the road changed was not simple. The state highway commission must first be persuaded to recommend the closing of the existing road. This they agreed to do after a new road Kanuga would construct was in place and had passed the state's inspection. The state's agreement with Kanuga was for Kanuga to have the road planned, engineered, approved and built first. At that point, the state would take over paving the road, seeding the banks, and all the other tasks necessary to complete the work. The state then, if all went as planned, would abandon the old road. The new road, just over one mile long, would divert traffic to Evans Road around the lake, thereby relieving the very serious hazard posed by the existing road running through the center of Kanuga. The cost to Kanuga for this construction was $275,000.

"Board of Visitors member Marie Colton of Asheville, a member of the state legislature, deserves almost total credit for the state's decision to help," Gooch said after the job was over.

The "Toms case" is one of the interesting sidelights of the history of Kanuga's land acquisition program. From the early days when there was no money—only good will—Kanuga had borrowed to acquire land to protect and enhance the original purchase. Several years before 1986, when Kanuga was low on capital funds, 200 acres which protrudes into Kanuga land just above the new cottages and includes Long Rock became available and board member Gayle Averyt bought the land personally to hold for Kanuga. Fred Toms in 1983 sued Kanuga, maintaining that he owned 50 of those acres. He had filed one lawsuit to block the exchange with the state of the new road for the old one, claiming that closing the old road to through traffic would have done him irreparable damage. The suit was dismissed on a technicality. He had previously represented himself in court, but for the Averyt property in question, he employed an attorney. The contending attorneys agreed that the acreage in question was not 50, but 43 acres, accepting Kanuga's surveyor data, and agreed to a $1,500 per acre price. Kanuga agreed to pay Toms $64,000 in exchange for a quit claim deed to Averyt for the 43 acres and all land Toms owned within one mile of the Inn. Averyt pledged the land to Kanuga when it became tax-advantageous for him to make the contribution. Had the case gone to court and had Toms won, the price of the land could reasonably have been more than $150,000. The secret in all this was that Kanuga lawyers thought Toms had a good case.

The property report to the board meeting in March 1986 was a virtual laundry list of capital improvements:

—*Work on the cottages was progressing*

—*Jackson Hall, the largest Grove classroom, was in operation as a year-round classroom giving Kanuga another 1,000 square feet of heated space.*

—*Work was underway to enlarge Baker Children's Building with another screened porch and some needed interior changes.* [This funding however, was from the William Garrett Skardon Baker Memorial Fund and from the Ahmanson Foundation of California.] *This building would be painted red and a bell installed giving the building an authentic little red schoolhouse appearance. In 1989, there were 203 children here during conferences, averaging about 40 per week.*

—*All of the old buildings at the Wildlife Camp were repaired, repainted, and some additional kitchen refurbishing was slated to be completed by summer.*

—*Eight more Inn rooms on the second and third floors were converted to private baths.*

—*The first floor of the Inn was completely repainted and carpeted.* [President Gooch, or Albert, as he was called by almost everyone, had apparently negotiated such a favorable carpet deal that it was referred to in the minutes as "the carpet Albert stole."]

While two buildings installed next to Cottage #15 were not stolen, they were "hand-me-down" gifts. Fred and Caroline Niehoff of Hendersonville, found themselves owners of two cottages that would have to be either moved or torn down to make way for construction on some property they had leased to a local bank. While smaller than Kanuga cottages in design—these were one- and two-bedroom—they were compatible with Kanuga cottages and small enough to be movable. They were moved.

In 1987 at Kanuga there were 121 primary buildings—with seven and one-half acres of roof to maintain for those interested in Kanuga trivia—located on about fourteen hundred acres. Phil Dietz reported that property had received more support on equipment needs in the last three years than in the first fifty. Since property management is directly related to use and growth, any time the question "where do we go from here?" is asked, space needs are again up for discussion. The question was formally asked and Richard D. (Dick) Austin chaired a committee to ask it in a sophisticated way—a Long-Range Planning Committee. It would cover every aspect of Kanuga. Its recommendations for buildings and grounds was that while some construction was anticipated, some renovations required, and always land purchases to be considered, maintenance and service would be preeminent. For perspective, Kanuga at this time ranked fifth in the capacity among the major Western North Carolina conference centers. Only giant Ridgecrest operated by the Southern Baptists and Lake Junaluska operated by the Methodists surpassed Kanuga in operating revenue.

The staff dining room, a memorial to long-time housekeeping head Gelola Johnson, was constructed in 1988-89. Located above the loading docks, it provided for the first time a staff dining room which could seat 60 and would permit the staff to eat in shifts during crowded times, which would better suit work schedules of various departments.

An extensive renovation, completed February 1989, of the summer-only dormitory for women summer staffers, called Fanny Hill, made the 1965 structure an all-season residence. This was a major project with about 325 square feet of space being added to an existing 2,880 square foot building and it was re-designed to accommodate both males and females. It would be an income potential in off-season months for youth groups. First to use the updated facility with the strange-sounding name were 20 firefighters with the United States Forest Service. The "Hotshot" unit prefers to train and study in the same place and in their bright orange slickers have returned to Kanuga each year since then. "Until you have made a proposal to the U.S. government, saying you will house its people in a place named Fanny Hill, you still have an experience ahead of you!" Gooch told the board.

The Kanuga staff got to know the firefighters and professed a great deal of respect for them and their professionalism. Their yearly continued use of Kanuga also helped provide steady income and work for food service and housekeeping staff members whose employment status often is tenuous during the early months of the year. Funding for this renovation was not from the capital fund, but from the Janirve Foundation of Asheville and Buddy and Sandy Carter, then of Pass Christian, Mississippi.

Accordingly, the building was renamed Carter Lodge.

Harold House, formerly Dingleberry, which was constructed in 1966 as a summer-time dormitory for male summer staff, was in early 1990 insulated and heated for year-round use. Phil Dietz did the design work and the $70,000 budgeted amount was, like the $85,000 spent on Fanny Hill, deemed both desirable and cost effective. The 30 Fanny Hill beds enabled Kanuga soon to book two large groups which otherwise could not have been accommodated. Those groups brought in $100,000. The two winterized dormitories increased the winter housing capacity ten percent.

Many of the improvements at Kanuga during this time either were not at first obvious or were not visible to many who came to Kanuga. The landscaping along the 30-row of cottages was effective because it was subtle. The Colhoun Room with its fireplace and the Michal Patio, constructed on the previously unfinished north side of the gym, have been used since first opened, and give the impression of having always been there. The gym addition extended the roof on the unfinished side to make an activities addition. Tennis courts with back fencing and paving and maintenance are expensive and are important to those who play tennis. Guests initiated round-robin tournaments in different years for the two different courts and raised $12,000 to solve the problem. Kanuga helped. The shuffleboard courts got a new look in 1993 with improvements made possible in honor of Robert T. Ashmore.

And while the water system at Kanuga was critical, the problem was not visible. Kanuga water came from springs. New state water-use regulations required all community water users to abandon the use of springs. Springs are in general more susceptible to carrying the amoebic matter giardia because they are close to the surface of the land. Hendersonville water would cost $200,000 to tap into; two wells would cost $25,000 with $5,000 more to cover the reservoir. Not surprisingly, the well driller was called.

Two prizes in the Kanuga crown—Camp Kanuga and the Wildlife Camp—initiated in considerable measure as revenue-enhancing services which the Kanuga philosophy could encompass, had evolved into an integral part of what was Kanuga. Accordingly, when additions were made to Camp Kanuga facilities the whole of Kanuga was enriched. Ditto with the Wildlife Camp.

Two major additions to Camp Kanuga were a new reception-staff building and an activities building. For the first time the camp had an enclosed meeting space for the whole camp. The activities building, a gift of Mrs. Harry Fox of Atlanta, dedicated June 29, 1988, was named the Fox Activities Building. The same 1988 dedication day, the camp dining hall was named Verduin Hall in honor of the builder of the camp. The plaque reads: "Honoring Willard P. Verduin, Planner and Builder of this Camp who, with his wife Evelyn served Camp Kanuga for Boys and Girls and Kanuga Conferences from 1950 to 1963." During this decade there was extensive landscaping at Camp Kanuga, a basketball court enlargement, plus the addition of tether ball areas and a volley ball court. The camp is built around Lake McCready, an artificial lake formed by a substantial dam. Interestingly, Camp Kanuga enrollment outpaces other registrations and each year the camp fills early.

Camp Kanuga Trailblazers Program was established for 16-year-olds and former campers, and features an eight-day back packing and camping trek along the Appalachian Trail. Sessions at the camp's rope course, white water rafting, and rock climbing are part of the popular program. Meg's Outpost, the new Trailblazer campsite, lies on a wooded hillside a quarter-mile from the camp proper.

A swimming lake for the Wildlife Camp was accomplished by providing Little Mud Creek that flows through the site with a deeper stream bed and also a dam which would raise the water level and form a lake. The stream was temporarily diverted to accommodate a large track-hoe which excavated some 40,000 yards of dirt. The dirt then was hauled up Evans road and deposited on another part of Kanuga property. The 1991 January through February winter did not cooperate. It rained all through those two months and there was mud everywhere—including mud on Evans road.

Kanuga seems to have dam-building problems. In 1929, when Kanuga was rebuilding Kanuga Lake dam the county officials complained about the dam construction's impact on the road below the dam. In 1991, local residents complained about the new dam construction's impact on the road.

An unanticipated large, deep rock formation in the center of the projected lake was too costly to move and was left in place. Fill dirt was added to create the small island in the lake.

The lake would be used by the National Wildlife Camp which leases the west camp facility from early June through mid-August. This would alleviate the overcrowding of the swimming area of Lake Kanuga when Wildlife campers came for their swim period. Named the Ned Ball Wildlife Park it honors former Kanuga board member, the late Ned Barclay Ball of Portland, Oregon, retired president of the Merrill Lynch Corporation.

In his "Letter to Friends" September 1992, Albert Gooch wrote: "If you have not seen that end of the campus lately, you simply must. It would be worth the trip. Standing by the St. Paul's-Colhoun Gym you can see the Michal Patio, Wilson Pond, the Barr Fitness Trail and Pinky Fields (playing fields) and the renovated Harold House. From there it is only a short walk down a wooded trail to the Ned Ball Wildlife Park which includes the Grace Ball Picnic Grounds and the Ned Ball Lake."

Not too far away is the recently completed (1988) renovation of The Grove as a memorial to Frederick (Bud) Minkler. Located adjacent to the Balthis program building, the Grove consists of five program buildings—Percival, Hunter, Jackson, Clarke, and Finlay halls. Jackson, Hunter, and Percival halls already had been renovated, insulated, and heated. Gifts from Bud's friends and from his family renovated Clarke and Finlay. In addition, the old bath house was converted to year-round modern facilities for men and women. Landscaping and lighting for the grounds plus laying out walking paths to the several buildings completed the project. The Grove would handle up to 260 guests and provide greater flexibility for varieties of space useful in program scheduling. The project required 100 loads of fill dirt, 150 tons of crushed granite, and 200 railroad ties. The desired aesthetic effect was achieved and it looks as if it had always been there.

"With the completion of the waterfront building, we have finished most of the major projects we have been talking about for so many years. I say most because we still have the staff recreation building and the storage building to consider," Albert Gooch had written in his March 1991 report to the board.

Constructing the waterfront, however, did not come to pass easily. The Edwin Voorhees pavilion watercolor sold in the bookstore was nostalgic of a milieu that included the sing-alongs with Mummy and Scotty Robertson and memories of Sadie

Watters and Mrs. Finlay. The question for many after the pavilion was dismantled was the form its replacement would take. It was in the plans. When the board considered the replacement question at its March 1990 meeting the anticipated favorable vote to accept the recommendation of the Property Committee to proceed with replacement plans was not to be. One bishop "had reservations" about the pavilion but did think the proposed dock area was needed. Gooch introduced a compromise suggestion—that the board authorize rebuilding the docks and that a committee be formed to explore the possibilities of donors to pay for the pavilion. The vote passed, but again was not unanimous, unlike most Kanuga board votes.

A firm commitment of $75,000, with the assurance from that donor of assistance in helping raise the balance necessary, turned the idea around. With money from the development fund and other unrestricted accounts that could be committed with Executive Committee approval and a committee willing to raise the balance, a second proposal was ready for the Board of Directors. The favorable vote came in October 1990, but again it was not a unanimous vote. The Cuningham Pavilion was dedicated when the Board of Visitors met at Kanuga in October the following year.

Describing the building at summer's end Gooch wrote: "What a difference the Cuningham Pavilion has made to Kanuga life. With its enlarged swimming area, there is plenty of room for inner tube floaters, lap swimmers, and active children. The sun deck provides lots more room and the adjacent rest rooms are a real convenience."

Promotion and Finance
1983–1993

Kanuga in 1983 received a bequest of $50,000 as the initial portion of a gift which would in time total over $75,000. It was the largest gift made by a single individual up until that time. The gift came from the estate of Stephen F. McCready of Ocala, Florida. McCready's interest in Kanuga stemmed from the years when his father was rector of Trinity Church, Asheville. He made many gifts to Kanuga over the years. He had a particular interest in youth programs and provided funds for many to attend conferences and the Guest Period—and the lake at Camp Kanuga was named in his honor.

This McCready gift epitomizes Kanuga giving: a long-time Southern constituent giving to the Kanuga he has over many years come to know and to love. A collage of statements puts into focus the promotional dilemma of the decade ahead, that is, preserving that which had come to be Kanuga while at the same time acknowledging its position of becoming a national institution. The director of promotion acknowledged the difficulty when he said, "While holding on to our constituency, we must expand into new areas." And commenting on growth, President Gooch observed: "Another danger in growth is the possibility of losing the close, intimate, caring touch for which Kanuga has long been famous." This close, intimate, caring relationship is amplified in Gooch's comment on the success of the bookstore after it had been reorganized as a Kanuga operation: "This is due to Sara Dudney's enthusiasm—plus the fact that she knows practically everyone who walks into the store, or at least somebody in their family." Further, recognizing and accepting the dilemma Gooch wrote: "Reaching out to the Episcopal church across the nation, we must always remain aware of our home folk—those who stood by us year after year and deserve to share in this success."

In 1983, a total of 13,410 guests spent 48,489 guest days at Kanuga; in 1984, the figures were 15,604 and 54,615; and in 1986, a bit over 16,500 and over 63,000. There were many reasons for this increase. First, however, has to be the slate of conferences put together by the Program Committee. Second, the message got out. The message got out directly by carefully prepared promotional materials; it got out also through an informal network of what perhaps is best described by Joe Cumming (Joseph B. Cumming, Jr., son of attorney Joseph Cumming), when he told a Kanuga homecoming gathering, "Kanuga makes one small town of all the South."

In April 1984, the practice of recognizing every person and parish making a gift to Kanuga the previous year was formalized in the *Kanuga News* (the previous 1974 attempt to recognize annual giving had been discontinued). In 1985, slide shows and videotapes were produced for effective advertising. These presentations were professionally produced for Kanuga through media specialists on loan from the Colonial Life and Accident Insurance Company, courtesy of its chief executive office and Kanuga board member, Gayle Averyt. Extensive advertising appeared in *The Episcopalian, The Christian Century, The National Catholic Re-*

porter, and *The Living Church.* The old standbys, program cata-
logues, camp brochures, and parish kits, continued to serve their
proven useful purposes. This promotional pattern of advertising
was continued throughout the decade and is the core of today's
Kanuga promotional effort.

The concurrent network route of getting out the news can be
described by two stories. First is a story printed in *The Delta*, the
news magazine of Sigma Nu, an undergraduate college social
fraternity. On the front cover of the 1991 fall issue is a picture of
the dedication of the Ned Ball Wildlife Park at Kanuga. The
Kanuga story is the major focus of the issue. A feature of the article
is a reprint of Charles Thomas' many years earlier report to *The
Delta* about his early Kanuga days setting up the canteen. There
are pictures restating the Sigma Nu-Sewanee-Kanuga connection of Bishop Thomas Wright; Presiding Bishop of the Episcopal
Church, John Hines; the 1929-1939 editor of *The Delta*, Charles
Thomas; and Ned Ball. The story recognizes Albert Gooch "for his
major contribution to this story."

Another example of networking is the fund-raising for the
waterfront building. The board authorization was to build when
funds were in hand. "That plan moved ahead rapidly when Sally
Bet and Jack Nevius of Washington, D.C., and her father J. Wilson
Cuningham of Winston-Salem, pledged over one-half the total
needed. Several other calls produced sufficient pledges and we are
now only about $25,000 from our goal," Gooch related.

Cottages were refurbished through a planned promotional
endeavor that asked individuals and parishes to assume financial
responsibility for an identifiable part of Kanuga—a cottage.
Between 1983 and 1989 Kanuga had put over $1 million into
maintaining the old Richard Sharp Smith green cottages. Kanuga
was in 1993 to learn that it was because of preserving these
historically significant buildings that Kanuga was eligible for
recognition on the National Register of Historic Places. The
promotional program was for individuals or parishes "to adopt" by
providing the necessary endowment for long-term preservation.
It was estimated that $5,000 per cottage or some $240,000 capital
investment would provide sufficient income for long-term preservation. Advertising was kindred to real estate sales with cottages
pictured and then "adopted" printed across the picture like "sold"
in house sales when the necessary funding was in hand. Recog-

nition was given to the donor.

The Property Committee in 1987 observed "that Guest Period people loved to be elegantly shabby but conferees came for learning in comfort." Guest Period people in 1983 raised money to construct The Guest Services Building. Board member Edward K. Pritchard, Jr., led the drive and Charleston people raised about one-third of the funds and the board added the rest to complete primarily a laundromat and rest room facility down by the tennis courts. Guest Period people at Kanuga have always assumed a kind of proprietary ownership that is not encouraged in many diocesan conference centers. When some adults substituted music for Kanuga's bugle calls, Luke Zannoni circulated a petition and the bugle call was back on the loudspeaker. Luke was at Kanuga with his father, Arthur E. Zannoni, a conference keynoter. When stories like the building of the Guest Service Building and the petition of Luke's are printed in Kanuga promotional material, this proprietary ownership is encouraged.

Kanuga has profited from this shared ownership in ways big and small. Thanks to the "Fan Club," a group of 89 persons and families who contributed to a special fund, each of the Inn's 63 guest rooms got ceiling fans. The "Fan Club" was launched when two good friends offered a $5,000 challenge gift. It grew to $12,000, the cost of fans plus the installation. Alice and Eldred Kuppinger had a monogrammed silver tea service which they wished to retire as they were retiring from years in the U.S. Foreign Service. The "K" was also the monogram for Kanuga where it now does service. A drive for sterling spoons to go with the tea set brought in 42 spoons. "Kanuga makes one small town of all the South."

The president's report to the board in 1985 identified three development goals for Kanuga: to keep fees and rates reasonable; to be able to offer scholarship assistance to those who need it; and to keep the facilities in good repair, safe, comfortable, and inviting. To achieve this, Kanuga would need a continuing flow of unrestricted gifts each year, money that could go into a pool for those purposes in contrast to money given for a designated building or maintenance purpose. President Gooch stated that ten percent of the operating budget would be required to achieve those goals. During the two years of the Capital Funds Campaign, the unrestricted Annual Fund was only $75,000—down about $50,000—

which was attributed to the two campaigns running concurrently. But once past the campaign, the Annual Fund drive would be a fact of Kanuga life.

The 1991 Annual Fund was $227,000; in 1992, it was $229,786. The 1992 number of donors was 1,548, an increase of 881 from the 667 recorded in 1983. The year 1992 ended a ten-year period during which time gifts to Kanuga totaled $5,663,411, an average of $566,341 each year.

In 1989, Kanuga proposed a plan to raise an endowment fund of $1 million to generate approximately $80,000 which would be used yearly for designated purposes related to the overall Kanuga mission. Kanuga's annual budget in 1989 was just over $3 million.

In place also at this time were three endowments: (1) The Hartley Endowment, begun as part of the earlier capital fund campaign supporting the efforts of the Program Committee; (2) the Kanuga-Garrett Baker Memorial, which chiefly provides for children's and young people's programs, with a portion used to maintain and equip the Baker Children's Building and sponsoring an annual preschool/parenting conference; and (3) the Bowen Endowment, which sponsors a yearly-Christian commitment conference. The cottage maintenance fund also was in the works, though not completed, with about a quarter of a million dollars. The 1989 endowment proposal would set up two legal endowment corporations with separate boards to invest and manage the funds.

In 1991 two separate legal endowment corporations, each with a board, were established. The Kanuga-Garrett Baker Memorial, Inc. and the Kanuga Endowment, Inc. would permit each board to pursue different investment strategies and at the same time provide that Kanuga operations would not be at risk should adverse earnings affect either investment. In the Kanuga Endowment, Inc. the 1989 distribution goal of the following amounts was achieved: $100,000 Christian Education Conference; $80,000 Guest Period Chaplains' Program; $100,000 Camp Kanuga including scholarships for the camp; $200,000 Scholarship, with naming opportunities available for gifts of $5,000 or more; $270,000 Cottage Maintenance; $100,000 annual winter conference—the successful Bowen Christian Commitment Conference; and, $150,000 Facilities Maintenance.

The distribution of earnings would be allocated on the basis of funds in the separate accounts. That is to say, the Christian Education Conference fund could be designated for contributions by those interested in this particular activity, and depending on the stock earnings, more funds would be available each year to commit to that conference.

The endowment boards would manage additions to the established endowments. An example is the foundation grant in 1992 for $5,000 and matched two-for-one by friends of Paul Martin which created the Paul Martin Memorial Art Fund, adding $15,000 to the Kanuga endowment. Eighty-four families and friends gave to the memorial. Earnings will be used to help fund the Guest Period art program.

In early 1993 the two endowment portfolios each contained over $1 million. One recent major addition to the endowment fund honors the living—Merrilyn and Phil Dietz. When Merrilyn retired in 1992 as Kanuga's dining room supervisor, the board sought a way to pay tribute to her and to Phil for their combined nearly half-century service to Kanuga. The board authorized an endowment of $50,000 in their honor and would name the large dining room at the Inn "The Dietz Room" when the funds were in place. Working quietly, the goal was surpassed and then an anonymous donor agreed to give the last $15,000 once a total of $85,000 was reached. The most-used room at Kanuga has in place an endowment of over $100,000.

For those who manage Kanuga, their efforts all seem to be amply rewarded when a letter like this can be shared with the Kanuga constituency:

Fran and I have come back to Kanuga again as we have, often several times a year, since we both were children here. We come because we know that we will see once more friends from other times and other places. We look forward to sharing with them worship and conference experiences, and to spending leisurely hours along the wooded trails or in casual porch conversations. [2]   *Syd Alexander*

Personnel
1983–1993

In the legends of early Kanuga there is a story that illustrates the unbelievable informality of another day. It is told by Emmet

Gribbin who during the 1930s worked in various summer jobs from the time he was a senior in high school on through college:

> *One summer we rented the facilities to the Lutherans for a week. Most of us on the permanent staff stayed to operate the place. Something happened that we didn't have a nurse for two days. I put on a tie and ran the infirmary until Mr. Morgan [Rufus Morgan] could get a nurse. When people came in to complain of a headache or something, I would say, "Go get into bed and take it easy." I was mighty relieved when the nurse arrived. All my patients survived.*

Today also, Kanuga employs summer staff. The job description of these positions tells an interested reader what is happening at Kanuga in the summer.

Conference Center jobs:

—*Registered nurses (RN) preferred but not required*

—*Children's program director, to supervise a staff of six. Degree in pre-school education preferred*

—*Children's program staff, minimum age 18*

—*Youth program coordinators, develop and direct youth programs for recreation, education, and spiritual enrichment.*

—*Chaplain's assistant/sacristan, related experience such as altar guild is essential. Must be good at piano or organ.*

—*Camp cooks, to cook meals at one of three kitchens*

—*Camp head chef/managers, for either of two camp kitchens*

—*Bus driver, school bus driving experience preferred*

—*Driver/mail clerk*

—*Lifeguards, lifeguard training certificate required. Minimum age, 18*

—*Kitchen workers, dining room staff, grounds keepers, staff, minimum age 16*

Camp Kanuga jobs:

—*Camp counselors, men and women. Live in cabin with campers, plan and direct programs. Skills needed in one of the following: aquatics, arts and crafts, rock climbing/ rapelling, archery, team and individual sports, camping/ backpacking, environmental studies, drama and dance*

—*Performing arts director, to direct drama and dance programs for campers*

—*Rock climbing instructor, experienced persons to instruct and direct rock climbing classes and trips on and off the camp property*

—*Environmental education specialists, to coordinate and instruct environmental classes and special environmental projects. College degree preferred*

—*Outdoor living skills instructor, to develop and implement outdoor living skills and classes. College degree preferred*

—*Waterfront instructors, must have WSI/lifeguard training*

—*Aquatics director, must have WSI/lifeguard training. Responsible for supervising swimming and boating program, waterfront instruction*

These jobs have been defined by Kanuga as more than summer jobs. These mostly high school and college age young people live together at Kanuga and the building of community within the staff is a goal. Summer-staff program coordinators plan daily activities for after-working hours that include informal sports, cookouts and campouts, theme parties, dances, movie nights, and other ideas that may originate either from the staff or the group. A staff council is elected to handle issues within the summer staff community. A weekly worship service is scheduled for the summer staff. Most conference center personnel are housed in separate men's and women's dormitories and they receive room and board as part of their pay. Some summer personnel are hired for only one month to give others a chance to work at Kanuga. Bishop Finlay early found that it was necessary to spread the summer jobs around by similar time period restrictions. Dorothy Crawford, Bishop Finlay's long-time secretary, records that she was constantly besieged by tearful young people on staff to "please let me stay just one more week."

"In a story of Kanuga there are many whose names should be mentioned for the splendid contributions they have made. I recognize how dangerous it is to single out a few," Bishop Finlay wrote in his reminiscences of early Kanuga. There were those whose presence was such that they became legend. "One of the wonderful people I have known at Kanuga was Miss Julia Betty Drake. Without her we could not have run the place. She had been at Kanuga before the church bought the property...[and] was in charge of the general housekeeping," Emmet Gribbin remembered. When Gelola Levi Johnson died in 1988, after serving Kanuga as head of housekeeping for more than a quarter of a century, she too had become a legend. "Throughout all those years, Gelola looked upon Kanuga as 'home' and kept it neat and clean for all her guests," Frank Ballard remembered.

Just as Albert Gooch was arriving at Kanuga in 1983, program director LaRue Downing was leaving Kanuga to return to the parish ministry in Augusta. Both the board and Gooch were in agreement that Gooch take time to get thoroughly on top of his new responsibilities before hiring a replacement for this job. Caroline Hughes was the Program Committee chairperson and with the existing staff continued the program work until her tenure in that committee assignment ended in 1985. The board commended her for her work saying that she was effective because she was "aware of Kanuga's dreams and also understood the practical side and brought both to bear on decision making." She was followed in that committee assignment by the new Program Committee chairman who also was the suffragan bishop of the Diocese of Upper South Carolina, Rogers Harris. In mid-March 1987, Lucia Randolph Townsend was selected as program director for Kanuga Conferences.

The Townsend appointment was made through a screening committee with the president making the final choice. While the individual would work with the Program Committee, the final responsibility for his/her effectiveness was with the Kanuga president. During the years when the position was vacant, the staff divided the work load to accommodate the work that Townsend would take up. At the time of her appointment she was coordinator for the ministry on aging at Christ Church, Greenville, South Carolina. She had studied music education at Converse College. Also Rannie, as she was called from the very first day, had had a long association with Kanuga. She had been a camper, counselor and staff member, and had organized programs at Kanuga for her parish.

Two of the most visible people on the staff are the camp director and the conference center guest services director. After ten years as counselor and associate director, and four years as director of the camp, Jerry Courtney resigned to take a job in conference center central management. The announcement of his leaving was not made until the end of the 1985 season. He wanted the camps to be memorable for the students and knew knowledge of his leaving could not contribute to the camp goals he set. Mike

Norman replaced Courtney. He was a cum laude Tennessee Technological University, A.B., M.A. graduate. He also had prior Kanuga experience and had several distinguished teaching years in Georgia behind him. Ability to work with young people is an absolute in this job. Since this ability is related to age, turnover in this job is expected. In 1989, Joe Britt became Camp Kanuga's new director. He came to the job with thirteen year's experience in training, counseling, teaching, and ministering to young people. He is a 1976 graduate of Presbyterian College with a degree in religious studies and teaches religion at Christ Church Episcopal School, Greenville, South Carolina. Joe directs the five summer camp sessions, has the responsibility of staff selection and is Kanuga's liaison with the American Camping Association.

Hoyle Adams is full-time guest services director. He has had this job since May 1990. He is from Hendersonville and has a degree from the University of North Carolina at Charlotte. His department is in charge of meeting the logistical needs of user groups—meeting space, audio/visual equipment, social hours, and coordinating schedules. Staffing is part-time and seasonal. Prior to Hoyle's term, many of these duties were handled by Mike Cogsdale, and then later by Tom Black and Cathy Bouggy.

Ridgeway "Sandy" Lynch returned to Kanuga in 1987. Sandy first came to Kanuga in the fall of 1974. He was superintendent of property and maintenance until 1982 when he left to go into the firewood business using the wood splitter he had invented and had used to Kanuga's advantage for several years. Frank Ballard once said he could fix anything and keep it operating. "He was good with people and things—a tremendous attitude—ideally suited for Kanuga," Ballard told this writer.

Frank Ballard in 1987 resigned as promotion director to pursue a different professional goal—WSPA Radio as accounts executive. His years had been happy both for himself and for Kanuga. Clark Plexico replaced Ballard. Plexico was from Valdese, North Carolina, and was a graduate of The University of the South, Sewanee, where as a student he had worked with Gooch in the college admissions office. He knew both Kanuga and the Episcopal church well. Internationally minded, he stressed the need for Kanuga to become more ecumenical and more international in focus. He was active in North Carolina politics and had a vast knowledge of leaders throughout the state. "I am constantly amazed at how little is known about us with the non-Episcopalians in this area," he wrote in one of his annual reports. He held the job for two years and resigned to pursue graduate studies in Arabic languages. Plexico has served in the North Carolina Senate since 1990.

At the spring meeting of the Board of Directors, 1989, Phil Dietz and Ray West were each honored with titles of vice-president. Dietz was named vice-president/property and West named vice-president/administration. Board president Bishop William Weinhauer said that board members had voted to change the men's titles as a show of appreciation for their service to Kanuga. Although not observable to Kanuga guests there is also another titled person at Kanuga—"officer of the day." One Kanuga staff member is daily on constant call as a problem-solver and trouble shooter. Ray West, who is also a reserve United States Navy Commander, had early in his tenure adopted and adapted this traditional military title to identify the person on call.

Emily Heyward Freeman replaced Plexico in 1989. Freeman is another Kanuga YP (Young People's Conference) participant, dining-room summer staffer, and return-to-Kanuga individual. She also has achieved a Randolph-Macon Woman's College degree and several successful years of advertising and marketing research experience in the intervening years. Her department continues to produce brochures, press releases, and advertisements. The numbers today are staggering: 91,500 brochures were printed for the twelve 1991 summer offerings. Beyond pulling Kanuga constituency targeted for each conference, sixty outside lists were used or organizations contacted, including other Episcopal groups, other denominations, schools, and non-profit groups. A new Kanuga video was completed in 1991. Each summer she is assisted by a photography intern—most recently from the Rochester Institute of Technology.

Camps and Conferences
1983–1993

"The Program Coordinating Committee developed an attractive array of summer conferences for 1983," Albert Gooch, Kanuga's new president, reported. "Has any Episcopal conference center had the likes of O'Driscoll, Westerhoff, McNutt, Stendahl, Fenhagen, Peck, Sanford, the Friends of the Groom in one season—to say nothing of author Larry Packard keynoting a Youth Leaders Conference, John Palarine's highly successful Winterlight, or the PreSchool Education Conference?"

The successful conference format seemed to be in place and the 1985 schedule beginning June 9 would utilize five summer weeks like this:

Week #1 *Junior Young People's Conference, grades 6–8*
         Senior Young People's Conference, grades 9–12
         Adults working with Youth

Week #2 *Bible Conference*
         School of Prayer
         Clergy Couples Skills Conference
         Evangelism, Congregational Development in the
             Small Church

Week #3 *Province IV Youth Leadership*

Week #4 *Kanuga Renewal Conference*
         PreSchool/Parenting I

Week #5 *PreSchool/Parenting II*
         Christian Education Conference
         Church Arts Conference

The Church Arts Conference would conclude July 12 and the Summer Guest Period would begin the next day and would schedule guests through August 24. Late August and early September would be open for specially-scheduled conferences until mid-October when See The Leaves would be scheduled for about two weeks. Winterlight would fill the facility just after Christmas. Winterlight brings young people in grades 9–12 to Kanuga just after Christmas, December 27–January 1. Since its start in 1976, it has been very popular. Winterlight XVIII is expected once again to be filled to capacity. Small group discussions dealing with concerns of teenagers, games, sports, New Year's Eve Eucharist followed by a high-energy party and dance is a format that ensures success. Kanuga has carefully-chosen coordinators for this event and they are supported by an experienced staff of young people and adults.

Virtually the whole of the year was filled with the exception of Easter, Thanksgiving, and Christmas Day itself. Some board members and Albert Gooch also were aware of the possibility of using Kanuga for the traditional holidays and especially for those who for whatever reason were alone and would prefer to be with others at that time. Begun in 1986, Thanksgiving Guest Period (Wednesday supper through Sunday brunch) offered families the opportunity for reunion among good friends—where no one had to cook or wash dishes. A series of program activities was provided with services in the chapel Thanksgiving morning. The traditional turkey, dressing, and all the trimmings followed. This was an idea just waiting to be announced. The first year saw 220 gathered for dinner and friendship and the event grew until it was a full-house affair and early registrations today are a must. In 1992, the number of guests was 358.

Gifts in 1985 from the Bishop White Parish Library Association and from the Church Periodical Club of Province IV provided the financial impetus for the Kanuga library which was opened in April of that year with 483 catalogued volumes. Betsy Thomson provided the personal impetus and after her death one of the rooms was named in her honor—The Elizabeth Willcox Thomson Room. Also, in June 1985, Kanuga became a full member of the Council on Continuing Education Units and could offer CEU credits for many of its conferences.

Mid-point in the 1980s there was an upbeat in the Kanuga conferences that is difficult to encapsulate. Reporting on the vestry leadership conferences which Kanuga had sponsored annually since 1982, Albert Gooch in October 1986 told the board: "After years of mediocre attendance, we now have the right program format and—perhaps as important—the right dates." It was now on course late in January with "virtually every bed and every meeting room filled." The first "Thanksgiving at Kanuga" was especially successful and plans were in place for an ecumenical symposium that would deal with Christian faith and young children.

The Symposium on Faith Development in Young Children was scheduled for December 8–12, 1987. Coordinated by Furman professor Doris Blazer, who also was the director of Kanuga's effective PreSchool/Parenting conferences, the symposium brought some of the nation's foremost persons in the field as principal speakers. Participants came from 33 states and several countries. Grants totalling $75,000 from Ahmanson Foundation of California, Trinity Church of New York City, and from several interested friends underwrote the effort. Videotapes of the major addresses were produced, and Kanuga later produced a major book from the conference. *Faith Development in Early Childhood,* edited by Doris Blazer, was published in 1989 by Sheed and Ward, a service of National Catholic Reporter Publishing Company, Inc.

The Kanuga statement of purpose, revised in 1987, stated:

> *To provide for God's people in this broken world a glimpse of the Kingdom through hearing the Gospel, experiencing Christian community and being empowered for strength, growth and service in both our individual communities and in the rest of God's creation.*

This statement was interpreted to make program the main emphasis at Kanuga for the next five years. Kanuga would expand programs to attract persons of various races and socio-economic backgrounds, pursue programs in the broad areas of Christian concern that Kanuga programs in the past had pursued, and target special areas of Christian concern where Kanuga programs could be expected to make a contribution. Further, a Christian emphasis would be accentuated at Camp Kanuga, and chapel services would be regularly scheduled and would not be dependent on conference planned schedules. Bibles would be found in every room and Kanuga would work to strengthen its church relationships.

In 1987, 23 percent of the campers at Camp Kanuga were there with scholarship aid. The scholarship program grew throughout the decade. In 1989, Kanuga provided over $50,000 in scholarship aid; in 1990, $73,000; in 1991, $70,000; in 1992, $74,470. Late in 1989, President Gooch formally responded to criticism that Kanuga was too pricey and scholarship information was not well publicized. "By comparison with comparable camps in Western North Carolina, our rates are extremely reasonable. It is clear that we are catering to parents with income somewhat below those who send their children to privately-owned camps which offer programs not much (if any) better than ours. In addition we offer an incredible number of scholarships, available to anyone with genuine need.... Scholarship aid is primarily for camp, conference, and parish family weekends, but Kanuga has occasionally offered scholarship aid for Guest Periods when there is a special need," Gooch added in the same statement.

The cost of producing conferences increased during the decade of the 1980s. Keynoters came to expect greater honoraria, coordinators and staff expected more, and Kanuga put more money into planning meetings. Guest Period was in many ways the Kanuga bargain. Accepting the premise that Guest Period is a vacation and that vacations cost money, Kanuga for a family of four in 1989 averaged $43.50 per person a day. This included all meals and program. Today, there is no tipping at Kanuga.

In 1988, Camp Kanuga facilities were used in May before the scheduled camp session and again in August after the last scheduled camping session for Atlanta homeless children to experience camping. Kanuga board member Parker Hudson raised money for the May weekend and the second weekend was financed by several Atlanta Episcopal churches and the Episcopal Charities of Atlanta. Spartan Food Systems provided enroute meals at their Hardees in Lavonia, Georgia. There were 35 to 40 children each camping session, some of whom had never been out of the city before. A sobering part of the camp director's report to the board stated: "Until the children understood that there was plenty of food and would be for each meal, they wanted to hoard the food for another day." It has become an annual program with more cities, children, and programming involved.

The attention of the national church was directed to Kanuga in April 1988, when "Issues: '88 Conference on Human Sexuality and Women in the Episcopacy" brought together individuals with differing opinions at a time critical to the church. Special invitations were sent to persons chosen as diocesan deputies to the forthcoming General Convention of the church where those subjects would be further resolved. Two bishops, John S. Spong and William C. Wantland, addressed the sexuality issue; Bishop Wantland and the Venerable Denise Haines discussed the issue of women in the episcopate.

Later in September, the millennium of Russian Christianity was celebrated with a conference. In December, a Kanuga conference dealt with AIDS, the mentally ill, and the homeless. Both conferences were addressing issues that at the same time were very much in the national news. Not unlike the university president who frequently must respond in support of academic freedom, President Gooch said in response to some criticism about the issues conferences: "We believe that no matter how unpleasant controversies may be, Kanuga should provide a forum for fair and frank examination of such matters since they will affect the life of the church."

"Wonderful News!" was the heading of a memo to the Board of Directors, June 3, 1988. "Buford and Sally Bowen have today agreed to give Kanuga $100,000 to create the Bowen Endowment which will be used to sponsor an annual early spring conference on Christian Commitment.... The conference series, to be held some time during the first three months of each year, will concentrate on Christian commitment in a variety of areas, including but not limited to education, ethics, service, social concerns, missions, peace making, renewal, evangelism.... The intention is to make this a premier Kanuga conference of each year (very much like the Faith Development Symposium) with some of the most highly-respected persons in their fields invited to be keynoters." The Bowen Endowment Conference Committee which is appointed by the Kanuga board chairman administers the funds. Buford Bowen has been a Kanuga board member and both he and his wife have been members of the Board of Visitors. They recognized that such a conference could well change a low-occupancy month in which Kanuga lost $50,000 to $60,000 into, at the very least, a break-even month.

The Bowen Endowment funds were used first in February 1989 in a conference exploring the ethics of American corporate and public life. It was named "Connecting Sunday AND Monday." An array of speakers represented the public sector and the corporate sector. The co-author of *Habits of the Heart: Individualism and Commitment in American Life*, Robert N. Bellah, led the discussions with his book as the central focus. There were 167 participants from 23 states and the District of Columbia.[3]

The Bowen Endowment money was used in March 1990 to augment expenses when the church's national "Decade of Evangelism" was launched at Kanuga. Kanuga again had the attention of the leadership of the church when Presiding Bishop Edmond Browning with a host of speakers and 500 in attendance began the long-planned ten-year program about which Bishop Browning said: "There is nothing we will do in the nineties which will be more important than this." Videos of the major addresses of the conference were available from Robin Smith of Columbia, South Carolina, and his PhotoVision Company.

Very low-key was the 1989 "Christmas at Kanuga." They planned on 50 and had 170 in attendance. There were family groups, singles, divorced with children, recovering from death in the family, a 50-year-old newly-wed couple, and those who for reasons known but to themselves wanted companionship at Christmas. They temporarily became a family and sipped cider or whatever, made decorations and decorated a tree, packaged and delivered boxes of food and gifts for the needy, and then were able to simply walk across the way for the Christmas service.

The year 1990 was a banner conference year in important guests who participated in Kanuga conferences. Lord Donald Coggan, the 101st Archbishop of Canterbury, was one of the participants in the July Bible symposium. The very popular speaker and writer Madeleine L'Engle participated in the summer Reflections on Faith and Art Conference and "packed them in." An author of more than 40 books, she has become a Kanuga summer regular. The Bishop of Chicago, the Rt. Rev. James W. Montgomery, would have had the concurrence of her Kanuga following when he wrote: "Madeleine L'Engle has the ability to employ the insights of an artist in understanding the deepest implications of our life as children of God."

As conferences bring more and more people to Kanuga, questions of expansion again have been raised. President Gooch stated for the board that no expansion would be recommended by him. An optimal size seems to have been reached. A bit of expansion did, however, come in 1992 in time for the beginning of the summer conference season—the new Kanuga Bookstore. Located under the chapel for a number of years, it was moved to a new location opening off the lobby of the Inn. With additional space, more books were added as well as the Kanuga-logo sports and casual clothing. The bookstore is supplied by Education/ Liturgy Resources of Oxford, North Carolina, a company which provides books and gift items in variable quantities to institutions affiliated with the Episcopal church. This sales practice permits its clientele merchandise variety similar to that found in large bookstores. The Rev. Harrison Simons operates this enterprise as a ministry and directs profits back to Episcopal church causes. Sara Dudney, Kanuga's first full-time bookstore director, reports that the bookstore will sell books into the thousands of dollars when a popular author is a conference participant.

There was controversy at the 1991 Episcopal general convention in Phoenix that at times even became personal. The House of Bishops consequently scheduled a March 2, 1992, follow-up meeting and selected Kanuga as the location. It was a kind of reconciliation gathering and both the fact of the meeting and the formal letter at the conclusion of the meeting were national news-media stories. The Presiding Bishop later said, "Much of the success of our conference had to do with being at Kanuga." Another meeting of the House of Bishops was held at Kanuga in March 1993.

Late April and early May 1992, Kanuga was the host to a gathering of the church's international leaders. The 103rd Archbishop of Canterbury, the Most Rev. George Carey, chose Kanuga as the gathering place for the Standing Committees of Primates and the Anglican Consultative Council. About 30 committee members from all over the globe were in attendance. The purpose of the gathering at Kanuga was to set the agenda for the approaching January (1993) Joint Meeting of the Anglican Consultative Council and Primates in Cape Town, South Africa; to discuss the possibility of a Lambeth Conference in England in 1998; and to refocus and reflect on a sense of renewal that the church is experiencing. The Anglican Observer to the United Nations was present. Seven senior archbishops and bishops of the churches of the Anglican Communion were at Kanuga. (Chapter Notes identify the principal participants.)[4]

Like others who gather at Kanuga, the international guests enjoyed walks around the lake, informal meetings about the grounds, and one evening a social hour with the Kanuga board and Dr. Billy Graham, a nearby neighbor and friend of Archbishop Carey's.

It seems reasonable to conclude that the first editorial about Kanuga, an editorial printed in the Upper South Carolina diocesan paper *The Piedmont Churchman,* June 1932, is more applicable today than when the writer of that day wrote:

> *In a remarkably short time this venture* [Kanuga] *has become a virtual powerhouse for the educational and spiritual life of the church.*

That same editorial writer, the Rev. Albert R. Stuart of Greenwood, South Carolina, also concluded:

> *Let it* [Kanuga] *falter and become merely a recreational center with a suggestion of religion because* [it is] *sponsored by the Church, and that day our building ceases.*

There are today approximately one hundred Episcopal church diocesan camp and conference centers. Over 60 percent are year-round operations providing both camping and conference programs. The actual number is dependent on definition because a few are programs and not facilities. Fewer than 15 percent are operationally self-supporting and even those at times require financial assistance. The church's educational institutions—whether called church school, or college, or camp, or conference center—must depend upon supplemental income from their parishes, owning dioceses or through gifts from their constituencies in order to provide quality service at reasonable rates. Since its beginning as an Episcopal center, Kanuga has relied more heavily upon individual gifts from persons, families, and parishes than from the various dioceses. That support continues to this day, and is a very large part of the success story that has been Kanuga.

Camp and conference centers are part of the life of the Episcopal church. The camping experiences are inherently part of the youth leadership education program of the church. Dioceses are dependent on the conference centers for adult leadership training. These are the conclusions of the Rev. John (Jack) Andersen, executive director of the national church's association of Episcopal Camp and Conference Centers. Speaking from a ministry that has had its focus in interpreting and guiding these institutions, he also told this writer:

> Clearly Kanuga has set the direction and tone for camping and conferencing in the Episcopal church. Everywhere one goes you hear diocesan camp and conference center people say, "We would like to be another Kanuga."

ꗏ

Reference Notes
and Works Consulted

Index

Reference Notes

PREFACE

1. Wetmore, Ruth Y. *First on the Land.* Winston-Salem, North Carolina. John F. Blair, Publisher. 1957.
2. Mooney, James, *James Mooney's Historical, Myths, and Sacred Formulas of the Cherokees.* Asheville, North Carolina. Historical Images. 1992.
3. Powell, Williams S. *The North Carolina Gazetteer.* Chapel Hill, North Carolina. University of North Carolina Press. 1968.
4. Chiltoskey, Mary Ulmer. *Cherokee Words With Pictures.* Asheville, North Carolina. The Stephens Press. 1972.

CHAPTER ONE—A VISION

1. Introductory quotation is found in Bishop Kirkman Finlay's "Bishop's Address" to the first annual convention of the Diocese of Upper South Carolina, 1923. Episcopal diocesan convention proceedings are printed documents and are available primarily in Episcopal church seminary libraries and in diocesan archives.
2. The writer has attempted to tell the story of Kanuga as much as possible in the words and writings of the participants. Footnotes are omitted for readability since the documents quoted are available only in Kanuga archives. The documents are identifiable in context and are board minutes, committee reports, occasional papers, and *Kanuga News.*
3. Morgan, A. Rufus. "History of Kanuga," unprinted monograph. 1958. Kanuga archives.

4. Transylvania County, NC Record Book 51, page 303, August 11, 1925, documents the See Off property transfer. Parties to the purchase were Kirkman G. Finlay, W. H. K. Pendleton, and D. E. McCuen as trustees.

5. Morgan, A. Rufus. Letter relating author's memories at age 90 of early Kanuga camping experiences. 1979. Kanuga archives.

6. The bishops in addition to Bishop Finlay were Thomas C. Darst, Wilmington; Albert S. Thomas, Charleston; and Junius M. Horner, Asheville.

7. Starr, Homer W. *Believing Youth,* Milwaukee, Wisconsin. Morehouse Publishing Co. 1931. The book received favorable reviews the same year in *The Living Church, Religious Education,* and *The Churchman.*

Other Notes/Sources

8. The title "Mr." throughout the text is used as a clerical title only.

9. Tents used at the Tigerville camp were given to Mr. Pendleton by chaplains of the 27th New York Guard Division which trained at Spartanburg in 1917 and 1918. All were 50 by 25 feet and were in Kanuga service for many years.

10. Thomas, Albert Sidney. *A Historical Account of the Protestant Episcopal Church in South Carolina, 1820–1957.* Columbia, South Carolina. Printed by the R. L. Bryan Co. 1957.

11. London, Lawrence Fouchee, ed. and Sara McCulloh Lemmon. *The Episcopal Church in North Carolina, 1701–1959.* Raleigh, North Carolina. Printed by the Episcopal Diocese of North Carolina.

CHAPTER TWO—DREAM TO REALITY

1. The introductory quotation is from Bishop Kirkman Finlay's address to the convention of the Diocese of Upper South Carolina, 1928.

2. Articles in both the *Asheville Citizen* and the *Charlotte Observer* about George Stephens at the time of his December 15, 1943, death review the life of the North Carolina entrepreneur.

3. Finlay, Catherine "Bee," *Early Kanuga Memories.* The State Printing Company. Privately printed. 1976.

4. The first public announcement of the Kanuga Club was a long story prepared by W. W. Ball, obviously with the assistance of Stephens. It was printed both in the *Charlotte Daily Observer* and the *Charleston News and Courier*, October 11, 1908.

5. Bishir, Catherine W., ed. and Lawrence S. Earley. *Early Twentieth-Century Suburbs in North Carolina*, Privately printed, discusses John Nolen and includes references to his Kanuga work. 1984.

6. "Richard Sharp Smith," monograph, North Carolina Department of Cultural Resources, Asheville office, not dated.

7. Wood, Dorothy Kelley McDowell. *Gleanings from the French Broad Hustler, 1905–1910*, Hendersonville, North Carolina. Privately printed. 1991. The book is reprints of copies that now exist in North Carolina State Library, Raleigh, of Hendersonville's only newspaper during Kanuga's early years.

8. FitzSimons, Frank L. *From the Banks of the Oklawaha*, Vol. I. Hendersonville, North Carolina. Golden Glow Publishing Co. 1979.

9. Certificate of incorporation of the Kanuga Club filed March 4, 1919, in Office of North Carolina Secretary of State; certificate of incorporation of Kanuga, Inc., filed January 13, 1925; certificate of incorporation of Kanuga Estates, Inc., filed September 25, 1925, documents the financial plight of Kanuga during this time.

Other Notes/Sources

10. The General Alumni Association of the University of North Carolina, Chapel Hill, records contain a document accomplished by George Stephens, June 24, 1924, and the dates used in this text concerning Stephens are taken from this document. Newspaper documents vary in dates about Stephens' life.

11. Information about Stephens' athletic accomplishments and interests are found in a letter by George Stephens, Jr., February 23, 1981, to the Chapel Hill alumni director and contain quotations from the *Chapel Hill Weekly*, March 7, 1941.

12. *The Daily Tar Heel*, April 13, 1932, details George Stephens' thirty-two-year service to the Chapel Hill institution.

13. In the Oaks, Black Mountain, North Carolina, residence of Franklin Silas Terry, is listed on the National Register of Historic Places. Today, it is one of the conference centers of the Episcopal Diocese of Western North Carolina.

14. *Who's Who in America, 1926–1927*, reviews the Nolen accomplishments.

15. George Stephens continued his interest in Asheville real estate and bought Biltmore Village from the George Vanderbilt family and then began re-selling it to individual buyers during 1920 and 1921.

    Stephens was also a leader in the group which successfully championed the argument to Secretary of Interior Harold Ickes that the Smoky Mountain National Parkway should be located through the Western North Carolina side of the mountains.

CHAPTER THREE—EARLY YEARS

1. The introductory quotation is from a memorial address, January 24, 1939, at the 17th convention of the Diocese of Upper South Carolina by Bishop Albert S. Thomas.

2. Unedited manuscripts of the articles prepared for *Early Kanuga Memories* are on file in Kanuga archives.

3. Fletcher, Lucy. "Reminiscences of Early Kanuga." 1978. Monograph in Kanuga archives.

4. Phifer, Mary Hardy. *Kirkman George Finlay*. Chicago, Illinois. Manz Corp. 1949. Private printing. The only biography of Bishop Finlay.

Other Notes/Sources

5. Pendleton, W. H. K. "Bishop Finlay and the Spirit of Kanuga," 1948. Manuscript given to Kanuga by Mrs. Pendleton after her husband's death. In the manuscript Pendleton describes early diocesan camping efforts and efforts towards securing Kanuga property. Kanuga archives.

6. Reports to the Diocese of Upper South Carolina annually provide Bishop Finlay's description of Kanuga activities. Yearly reports to Kanuga Board of Managers provide financial details not contained in reports to the diocese. Kanuga archives.

CHAPTER FOUR—CHAPELS

1. The introductory quotation is the second stanza of an unpublished poem, "The Kanuga Chapel" by Helen Griffith, August, 1940. Helen Griffith also wrote the lyrics for "The Kanuga Song." The music for the song was composed by William G. "Scotty" Robertson. Marion Whatley, today a professional musician and one who in the 1960s worked at Kanuga, told the writer, "The Kanuga song is like a high school pep song, has an energetic tempo and words that evoke enthusiasm and loyalty. It gave a recognition to the strong feeling of community which existed there."
2. Finlay, Kirkman. "Kanuga," *Piedmont Churchman*, Vol. X, No. 3. 1932.
3. The writer interviewed Marguerite Alexander, daughter of S. Grant Alexander and a professional writer for the *Asheville Citizen*, at her home, Barnardsville, NC, July 2, 1992.
4. Author not credited, *Carolina Architecture and Allied Arts*, Miami, Florida. M. V. Publishing Co. 1940. Entrepreneurial publication which contains selected photographs of S. Grant Alexander's architectural work in the Asheville area.
5. Alexander, Marguerite, "Roots in Time, Grace Church Eyes New Era." *Asheville Citizen-Times*. Asheville, North Carolina. April 23, 1967.
6. The 1977 chapel renovation committee was composed of the Rev. Robert Haden, chairman, Mrs. Robert W. Polchow, the Rt. Rev. George M. Alexander, the Rt. Rev. William G. Weinhauer, and Ed Hartley.

Other Notes/Sources
7. *Highland Churchman*, Vol. XI, No. 5. May 1940, a publication of the Episcopal Diocese of Western North Carolina. Bishop Henry Center archives, Black Mountain, North Carolina.

CHAPTER FIVE—THE FORTIES

1. The introductory quotation by Berkeley Grimball is from the 1978 unprinted history of Kanuga prepared by Frank Ballard for the 50th anniversary celebration of Kanuga.
2. Walker, William L., editor. *Irascible Ol' Curmudgeon of Albermarle Point, The Wit and Wisdom of Berkeley Grimball.*

Charleston, SC. Porter-Gaud School. 1988. The book also contains a Kanuga Board of Directors' resolution of tribute to Berkeley Grimball which identifies the author of the quotation in greater detail.

Other Notes/Sources

3. A. Rufus Morgan was also the founder of the 1913 Diocese of Western North Carolina-sponsored Appalachian School where his sister, Miss Lucy Morgan, later in 1929 founded the Penland School of Handicrafts for the preservation of traditional mountain crafts.

CHAPTER SIX—THE FIFTIES

1. The introductory quotation is extracted from the Rev. John A. Pinckney's "The Report of the Superintendent of Kanuga Conferences," 1949. Kanuga archives. Pinckney in 1963 was consecrated bishop and served as bishop of the Diocese of Upper South Carolina from 1963 until his death in 1972.
2. The "Dear George" letter from Mr. Pinckney to board member Bishop George Henry, dated February 9, 1950; the letter from Mr. Capers Satterlee to Bishop Henry, dated November 22, 1950; and the letter to William L. Balthis from Bishop John J. Gravatt, dated November 22, 1950, are in the archives of the Diocese of Western North Carolina.
3. Campbell, Betsy. "Reminiscences of Early Kanuga Days." 1993. Monograph in Kanuga archives.

    The Rev. Alvin Skardon D'Aubert was the brother of Susan Baker for whom the Susan D'Aubert Baker Children's Building is named (dedicated to her, 1977). Father D'Aubert (1905–1981) was rector of the Church of the Good Shepherd, Houston, Texas, from 1944–1970.

CHAPTER SEVEN—BUILDING YEARS

1. The introductory quotation is from remarks made by Bishop George Henry to the Board of Managers; Board of Managers' minutes, July 8, 1963.
2. Officers of the Kanuga Episcopal Foundation were Ernest Patton, president; D. M. White, Jr., vice-president; James W. Marshall, Jr., secretary-treasurer; and Ed Hartley, Kanuga

executive director.

3. "Report of the Special Committee to Study Kanuga Confer-
    ences," 1964, was chaired by Bishop John A. Pinckney, with
    the document signed by John S. Spong, Ed B. Jeffress,
    Joseph Horn, Mrs. Robert Haden, and F. D. MacLean. John
    Shelby Spong was consecrated bishop in 1976 and has been
    bishop of the Diocese of Newark since 1979.

4. Reference file, Pack Library, Asheville. Newspaper name and
    publication date not included.

5. Speakers at "The Church Listens to the World and Responds"
    were Leon Modeste, John Wheeler, and the Rev. William
    Baxter. The "Family Conference" speakers were Ruth Cheney,
    Dr. Robert Wetmore, and the Rev. James C. Fenhagen.

CHAPTER EIGHT—INTERNAL DEVELOPMENT

1. The introductory quotation is found in a Program Committee
    document, "Kanuga Evaluation Procedures," presented to
    the Board of Managers, November 1969, written by the Rev.
    Hunt Williams. The Rev. Huntington Williams, Jr., was
    consecrated bishop in 1990 and has been since that date the
    suffragan bishop of the Diocese of North Carolina.

2. William Jones Gordon, retired bishop of Alaska, in conversa-
    tion with Jack Reak, at Kanuga, November 28, 1992, recalled
    austere early Kanuga camping days. Gordon was later on
    Kanuga staff and was on Kanuga Board of Trustees.

Other Notes/Sources

3. Kanuga archives has a collection of the public relations
    material used in the 1976 fund-raising campaign.

4. The main mast from the *USS Young D 580* was placed on
    permanent loan to Kanuga in 1970. The unexpected present
    came through the work of retired Rear Admiral Edwin J. S.
    Young who with his wife had earlier attended a Kanuga
    conference and had maintained an interest in the conference
    center. When the mast loan possibility became available he
    initiated the necessary correspondence between the Navy
    and Kanuga. The ship and the admiral only coincidentally
    bear the same name. The *USS Young* saw combat in the
    Asiatic Pacific fleet from 1942–1946. Yearly, Kanuga sends
    a report to the Navy stating that the mast is in good keeping.

5. Although five new Guest Houses were accounted for in 1982, a sixth cottage was completed in June 1984. It was the gift of Buford Bowen, given in memory of his daughter, Katherine Shepardson Bowen. Six cottages complete the cluster of Guest Houses.

CHAPTER NINE—TOWARD NATIONAL SERVICE

1. The introductory quotation is contained in "A Communiqué" from the Joint Standing Committee of the Anglican Consultative Council and the Primates of the Anglican Communion, April 30, 1992, meeting at Kanuga, and from a statement by the Most Rev. George Carey, Archbishop of Canterbury, *Kanuga News*, August 1992.
2. Syd Alexander, M.D., was director of the health services at the University of Alabama. He was at one time a member of the Kanuga Board of Directors and the Board of Visitors. His services to Kanuga were commemorated at the time of his death by a "Resolution of Appreciation" by the Kanuga Board, October 9, 1992.
3. Speakers at the February 1988 conference "Connecting Sunday AND Monday" in addition to Robert Bellah were Maria Campbell, John Boatwright, William Friday, and Manning Pattillo. Seminar leaders were the Rev. John Koenig, and Frank Alexander. The Rev. Roderic L. Murray was conference coordinator.
4. The primates in addition to Archbishop George Carey were the Most Rev. Brian Davis, Archbishop of New Zealand; the Rt. Rev. Samir Kafity, President-Bishop of Jerusalem and the Middle East; the Most Rev. French Chang-Him, Archbishop of the Church in the Province of the Indian Ocean; the Most Rev. Robin Eames, Archbishop of Armagh (Ireland); the Most Rev. Michael Peers, Archbishop of Canada; and the Most Rev. Edmond L. Browning, Presiding Bishop of the Episcopal Church in the United States. Two other archbishops present were the Most Rev. George Browne, Archbishop of West Africa, and the Most Rev. Douglas Hambidge, Archbishop of British Columbia. The Anglican Observer to the United Nations was the Rt. Rev. Sir Paul Reeves, former Governor General and Primate of New Zealand.

Acknowledgments

I want to express my appreciation first to Sarah McCrory who in 1988 as a volunteer put together the Kanuga archives. She did a great job organizing and making accessible material which almost defies classification. Second, appreciation is expressed to the Rt. Rev. Robert H. Johnson of the Diocese of Western North Carolina who permitted the temporary transfer of the Kanuga files in the archives of that diocese to the Kanuga archives during the year this book was in preparation.

Next, I want to thank a lot of people who were more helpful than any of them probably realize. Beginning with several bishops all of whom I now call friends, I received assistance from the Most Rev. John E. Hines; the Rt. Rev. William J. Gordon; the Rt. Rev. John S. Spong; and the Rt. Rev. Robert W. Estill. All are Kanuga alumni and all gave me both their time and encouragement. Other clergy also were helpful, especially the Rev. Emmet Gribbin of Northport, Alabama; the Rev. Robert L. Haden, Jr., of Charlotte; the Rev. L. Bartine Sherman of Hendersonville; and the Rev. Merrill Miller, Brevard.

Since most of the research was done by library and archival study, several professionals in different locations should be thanked: the Rev. John L. Janeway, Library of the School of Theology, The University of the South, Sewanee; Michelle Francis, Historical Foundation of the Presbyterian and Reformed Churches, Montreat; and Laura Gaski, Pack Library, Asheville. Elizabeth Holsten, General Alumni Association, Chapel Hill, was helpful in locating George Stephens' biographical information. Martha Fullington of the North Carolina Department of Cultural Resources guided me through the architectural review literature relative to Kanuga as a defined historically-significant site. Ruth

Y. Wetmore, Brevard College archaeologist, and George Frizzell, Special Collections librarian, Hunter Library, Western Carolina University, provided invaluable assistance in identifying relevant Cherokee literature.

Former Kanuga executive director Bill Verduin and his wife, Evelyn, were helpful. Frank Ballard continues his interest in Kanuga and shared information and ideas. I am especially indebted to him for information about ka-nu-ga which introduced me to the Cherokee linguistic material. Jody Barber who early took photographs of Kanuga provided information concerning Kanuga-related literature in the Hendersonville library.

Much help came from old and new friends. I remember especially Mrs. Mary Haden, Mrs. George Henry, and Mrs. Laura Abbott of Asheville; Mrs. Louise Bailey of Flat Rock; Emory Gash of Charlotte; Dr. Richard Alexander of Waynesville; the Hon. Robert Gash, and the Hon. Cecil Hill of Brevard.

All members of the Kanuga staff were helpful any time I asked for assistance. Ann McKinney was long-suffering in letting me interrupt her routine to answer questions, always with a smile. Sara Dudney volunteered to compile the index and review the bibliography and text. Albert Gooch is incomparable in editing and knows more about Kanuga than any person rightly ought to know. Emily Freeman is absolutely incredible in putting together a book. She can identify faulty reasoning or an inconsistency in paragraph structure like no one else. With all this help the book came together and somewhere along the way I began to use the pronouns *us* and *we* when referring to Kanuga. The errors of omission and commission are mine alone,

Jack Reak

Index

H

I